Learning QGIS

Second Edition

Use QGIS to create great maps and perform all the geoprocessing tasks you need

Anita Graser

[PACKT] open source

community experience distilled

PUBLISHING

BIRMINGHAM - MUMBAI

Learning QGIS

Second Edition

First published: September 2013

Second edition: December 2014

Production reference: 1031214

Published by Packt Publishing Ltd.
Livery Place
35 Livery Street
Birmingham B3 2PB, UK.

ISBN 978-1-78439-203-1

www.packtpub.com

Credits

Author
Anita Graser

Reviewers
Tsompanopoulos Efstratios (Stratos)
Min Feng
Daniela Pani
Cornelius Roth

Commissioning Editor
Amarabha Banerjee

Acquisition Editor
Larissa Pinto

Content Development Editor
Melita Lobo

Technical Editors
Tanvi Bhatt
Faisal Siddiqui

Copy Editors
Karuna Narayanan
Vikrant Phadkay

Project Coordinator
Sanchita Mandal

Proofreaders
Simran Bhogal
Maria Gould
Ameesha Green

Indexer
Priya Sane

Production Coordinators
Nilesh Bambardekar
Komal Ramchandani

Cover Work
Komal Ramchandani

About the Author

Anita Graser studied Geomatics at FH Wr. Neustadt, Austria, where she graduated with a Master's degree in 2010. During her studies, she gained hands-on experience in the fields of geomarketing and transportation research. Since 2007, Anita has been working as a geographic information systems (GIS) expert with the Dynamic Transportation Systems group at the Austrian Institute of Technology, where she focuses on analyzing and visualizing spatiotemporal data. Anita is a charter member of OSGeo and PSC member of QGIS. She has been working with GIS since 2005, and writes a popular blog on open source GIS at `www.anitagraser.com`.

I would like to say thanks to my family, partner, and coworkers for their support and encouragement. Of course, I also want to thank the whole QGIS community for their continued effort to provide the best open source GIS experience possible, and everyone who made the first edition of *Learning QGIS* such a great success.

About the Reviewers

Tsompanopoulos Efstratios (Stratos) has been balancing between Geodesy and GIS for the last 12 years. He is currently based in the Netherlands, working as an office surveyor and GIS Administrator for one of the world's leading surveying companies.

Stratos has a huge interest in GIS scripting and GIS databases and currently focuses on creating and maintaining the GIS database of his company while developing tools using Python. His future goals are to create comprehensive tools and several web applications for his company in order to improve work procedures.

When he is not concerned with "geeky stuff," Stratos tries to spend a lot of time with friends and family, listens to music, and travels as much as possible.

You can find more information about him at `www.linkedin.com/in/etsompanopoulos` or contact him at `stratos.tso@gmail.com`.

Min Feng completed his PhD degree in Cartography and Geographic Information Systems in 2008, and has worked at the Global Land Cover Facility (GLCF) at the University of Maryland, the Chinese Academy of Sciences (CAS), and United Nations Environment Programme (UNEP)'s Global Resource Information Database (GRID). He has been engaged in global high-resolution land cover and change research. He is an expert in high performance geospatial data processing, geospatial model sharing, and integrated simulation. His work has been published in top-ranking remote sensing and GIS journals. Feng is familiar with OGC/ISO standards and open source tools and libraries. He is also capable of programming using many languages, including C/C++, Java, Python, R, and IDL.

Born in Sardinia, **Daniela Pani** has a first degree in marine geophysics; a PhD in georesources geophysical exploration and a Diploma of the Imperial College in Remote Sensing. She has written more than 50 scientific papers on her fields of competence (RS, Geodesy, Geophysics, Cartography, GIS). In charge of two university courses, she's participated in numerous oceanographic cruises for seabed surveying, being part of the scientific groups for establishment of marine parks and land use regulations. She works in the Space industry and is currently a member of staff at the General Directorate of the Civil Protection for Sardinia. Daniela is a popular national/international speleologist and geoconsultant for a popular program on TV-RAI1.

Cornelius Roth holds a Master's degree in Geography and Geoinformatics at the University of Salzburg. He is currently working at the Department of Geoinformatics on research projects, helping them to use GIS-related methods in emergency and air traffic management, open source GIS, and Open data. Recently, he has also worked at the economic development agency BGL, Bavaria, with strong focus on fostering companies when applying GIS methods and services to support their business objectives. As a third pillar, he manages e-learning courses for the UNIGIS distance learning network in Salzburg.

www.PacktPub.com

Support files, eBooks, discount offers, and more

For support files and downloads related to your book, please visit www.PacktPub.com.

Did you know that Packt offers eBook versions of every book published, with PDF and ePub files available? You can upgrade to the eBook version at www.PacktPub.com and as a print book customer, you are entitled to a discount on the eBook copy. Get in touch with us at service@packtpub.com for more details.

At www.PacktPub.com, you can also read a collection of free technical articles, sign up for a range of free newsletters and receive exclusive discounts and offers on Packt books and eBooks.

PACKTLIB™

https://www2.packtpub.com/books/subscription/packtlib

Do you need instant solutions to your IT questions? PacktLib is Packt's online digital book library. Here, you can search, access, and read Packt's entire library of books.

Why subscribe?

- Fully searchable across every book published by Packt
- Copy and paste, print, and bookmark content
- On demand and accessible via a web browser

Free access for Packt account holders

If you have an account with Packt at www.PacktPub.com, you can use this to access PacktLib today and view 9 entirely free books. Simply use your login credentials for immediate access.

Table of Contents

Preface

Welcome to *Learning QGIS Second Edition*. This book will introduce you to QGIS 2.6 and teach you how to perform core geospatial tasks using this popular open source GIS. It takes you through six chapters, from the installation and setup of QGIS in the first chapter to the essentials of viewing spatial data in the second chapter. The third chapter covers data creation and editing followed by the fourth chapter that offers an introduction to performing spatial analysis in QGIS. In the fifth chapter, you will learn how to create great maps and how to prepare them for print, and the final chapter shows you how you can extend QGIS using the Python scripting language.

What this book covers

Chapter 1, Getting Started with QGIS, covers the installation and configuration of QGIS. You will also get to know the user interface and how to customize it. By the end of this chapter, you will have QGIS running on your machine and be ready to start with the tutorials.

Chapter 2, Viewing Spatial Data, covers how to view spatial data from different data sources. QGIS supports many file and database formats as well as OGC Web Services. We will first learn how we can load layers from these different data sources. Then, we will take a look at the basics of styling both vector and raster layers and create our first map. We will finish this chapter with an example that shows you how to load background maps from online services.

Chapter 3, Data Creation and Editing, covers the creation of new vector layers. Then, you will learn how to select features and take measurements before continuing with editing feature geometries and attributes. We will also reproject vector and raster data, and you will learn how to convert between different file formats before ending this chapter with joining data from text files and spreadsheets to our spatial data.

Chapter 4, Spatial Analysis, covers raster processing and analysis tasks such as clipping and terrain analysis. Then, you will learn how to convert between raster and vector formats before continuing with common vector geoprocessing tasks, such as generating heatmaps and calculating area shares within a region. Finally, we will finish the chapter with an exercise in automating a geoprocessing workflow using the QGIS Processing modeler.

Chapter 5, Creating Great Maps, covers important features that enable us to create great maps. We will go into advanced vector styling, building on what we learned in *Chapter 2, Viewing Spatial Data*. Then, we will cover labeling using examples of labeling point locations as well as how to create more advanced road labels with road shield graphics. You will also learn how to tweak labels manually. Finally, we will get to know the print composer, and you will learn how to use it to create printable maps and map books.

Chapter 6, Extending QGIS with Python, covers scripting QGIS with Python. We will start with an introduction to the QGIS Python console. Then, we will go into more advanced development of custom tools for the processing toolbox, and you will learn how to create your own plugins.

Who this book is for

If you are a user, developer, or consultant who knows the basic functions and processes of GIS but want to know how to use QGIS to achieve the results you are used to from other GISes, this is the book for you. This book is not intended to be a GIS textbook. You, the reader, are expected to be comfortable with core GIS concepts.

Conventions

In this book, you will find a number of styles of text that distinguish between different kinds of information. Here are some examples of these styles, and an explanation of their meaning.

Code words in text, database table names, folder names, filenames, file extensions, pathnames, dummy URLs, user input, and Twitter handles are shown as follows: "Use `[% $now %]` to insert the current time stamp."

A block of code is set as follows:

```
("landcover@1" > 0 AND "landcover@1" <= 6 ) * 100
+ ("landcover@1" >= 7 AND "landcover@1" <= 10 ) * 101
+ ("landcover@1" >= 11 ) * 102
```

When we wish to draw your attention to a particular part of a code block, the relevant lines or items are set in bold:

```
def initGui(self):
    # create the toolbar icon and menu entry
    icon_path = ':/plugins/MyFirstMapTool/icon.png'
    self.map_tool_action=self.add_action(
        icon_path,
        text=self.tr(u'My 1st Map Tool'),
        callback=self.map_tool_init,
        parent=self.iface.mainWindow())
    self.map_tool_action.setCheckable(True)
```

Any command-line input or output is written as follows:

```
sudo apt-get install qgis python-qgis qgis-plugin-grass
```

New terms and **important words** are shown in bold. Words that you see on the screen, in menus or dialog boxes for example, appear in the text like this: "You can increase your productivity by assigning shortcuts to the tools you use regularly, by navigating to **Settings | Configure shortcuts**."

> Warnings or important notes appear in a box like this.

> Tips and tricks appear like this.

Reader feedback

Feedback from our readers is always welcome. Let us know what you think about this book—what you liked or may have disliked. Reader feedback is important for us to develop titles that you really get the most out of.

To send us general feedback, simply send an e-mail to `feedback@packtpub.com`, and mention the book title via the subject of your message.

If there is a topic that you have expertise in and you are interested in either writing or contributing to a book, see our author guide on `www.packtpub.com/authors`.

Customer support

Now that you are the proud owner of a Packt book, we have a number of things to help you to get the most from your purchase.

Downloading the example code

You can download the example code files for all Packt books you have purchased from your account at `http://www.packtpub.com`. If you purchased this book elsewhere, you can visit `http://www.packtpub.com/support` and register to have the files e-mailed directly to you.

Errata

Although we have taken every care to ensure the accuracy of our content, mistakes do happen. If you find a mistake in one of our books—maybe a mistake in the text or the code—we would be grateful if you would report this to us. By doing so, you can save other readers from frustration and help us improve subsequent versions of this book. If you find any errata, please report them by visiting `http://www.packtpub.com/submit-errata`, selecting your book, clicking on the **errata submission form** link, and entering the details of your errata. Once your errata are verified, your submission will be accepted and the errata will be uploaded on our website, or added to any list of existing errata, under the Errata section of that title. Any existing errata can be viewed by selecting your title from `http://www.packtpub.com/support`.

Piracy

Piracy of copyright material on the Internet is an ongoing problem across all media. At Packt, we take the protection of our copyright and licenses very seriously. If you come across any illegal copies of our works, in any form, on the Internet, please provide us with the location address or website name immediately so that we can pursue a remedy.

Please contact us at `copyright@packtpub.com` with a link to the suspected pirated material.

We appreciate your help in protecting our authors, and our ability to bring you valuable content.

Questions

You can contact us at `questions@packtpub.com` if you are having a problem with any aspect of the book, and we will do our best to address it.

1
Getting Started with QGIS

In this chapter, we will install and configure the QGIS geographic information system. We will also get to know the user interface and how to customize it. By the end of this chapter, you will have QGIS running on your machine and be ready to start with the tutorials.

Installing QGIS

QGIS runs on Windows, various Linux distributions, Unix, Mac OS X, and Android. Also, the QGIS project provides ready-to-use packages as well as instructions to build from the source code at `http://download.qgis.org`. We will cover how to install QGIS on two systems: Windows and Ubuntu, as well as how to avoid the most common pitfalls.

> Further installation instructions for other supported operating systems are available at `http://www.qgis.org/en/site/forusers/alldownloads.html`.

Like many other open source projects, QGIS offers you a choice between a stable release version and the cutting-edge developer version, also called **master** or **testing**. QGIS master/testing will contain the latest and greatest developments, but be warned that on some days, it might not work as reliably as you want it to. For the tutorials in this book, we will use the QGIS 2.6 stable release.

Installing QGIS on Windows

On Windows, we have two different options to install QGIS: the standalone installer and the OSGeo4W installer. The standalone installer is one big file to download (approximately 260 MB for the 64-bit version and 320 MB for the 32-bit version); it contains a QGIS release and the **Geographic Resources Analysis Support System** (**GRASS**) GIS in one package. The OSGeo4W installer is a small, flexible installation tool that makes it possible to download and install QGIS and many more OSGeo tools with all their dependencies. The main advantage of this over the standalone installer is that it makes updating QGIS and its dependencies very easy. You can always have access to both the current and the developer versions, if you chose to, but of course, you are never forced to update. That is why I recommend that you use OSGeo4W. You can download the 32-bit and 63-bit OSGeo4W installers from `http://osgeo4w.osgeo.org` (or directly from http://download.osgeo.org/osgeo4w/osgeo4w-setup-x86.exe for the 32-bit version or `http://download.osgeo.org/osgeo4w/osgeo4w-setup-x86_64.exe` if you have a 64-bit version of Windows). Download the version that matches your operating system and keep it! In the future, whenever you want to change or update your system, just run it again.

> Regardless of the installer you choose, make sure that you avoid special characters such as German umlauts or letters from alphabets other than the default Latin ones in the installation path, as they can cause problems later on, for example, during plugin installation.

When the OSGeo4W installer starts, we get to choose between the **Express Desktop**, **Express Web-GIS**, and **Advanced** installations. To install the QGIS release version, we can simply select the **Express Desktop** option, and the next dialog box will list the available desktop applications, such as QGIS, uDig, and GRASS GIS. We can simply select QGIS, click on **Next**, and the download and installation will start automatically. When the installation is finished, there will be desktop shortcuts and start-menu entries for OSGeo4W and QGIS.

If we want to install QGIS master/testing, we need to go through the **Advanced** installation. This installation path offers many options, such as **Download without installing** and **Install from Local Directory**, which can be used to download all the necessary packages on one machine to later install them on machines without Internet access. It's usually not necessary to change the default settings, but if your machine is, for example, hidden behind a proxy, you will be able to specify it here. After the installer fetches the latest package information from OSGeo's servers, we get to pick the packages for installation. QGIS master/testing is listed in the desktop category as **qgis-dev**. To select it for installation, click on the text that reads **Skip**, and it will change and display the version number. The installer will automatically select all the necessary dependencies (such as GDAL, SAGA, OTB, and GRASS), so we don't have to worry about this. After clicking on **Next**, the download and installation starts automatically, just like in the Express version. The dialog will look like the following screenshot:

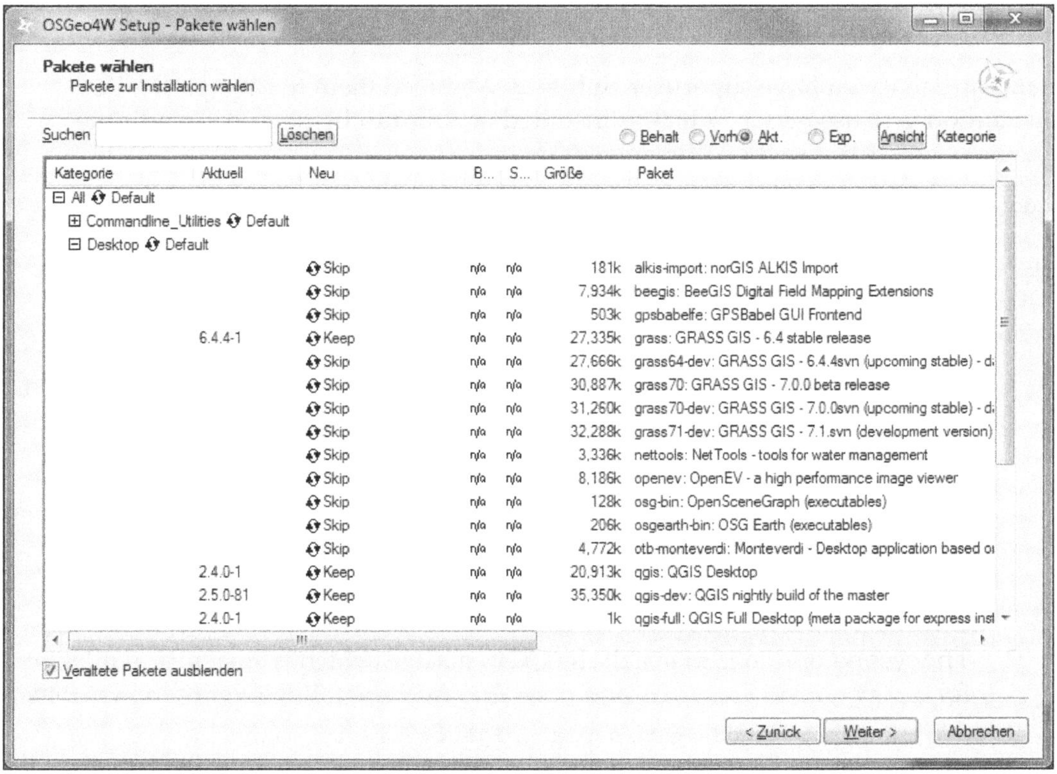

If you try to run QGIS and get a pop up that says, **The procedure entry point <some-name> could not be located in the dynamic link library <dll-name>.dll**, it means that you are facing a common issue on Windows systems: a DLL conflict. This error is easy to fix; just copy the DLL file mentioned in the error message from `C:\OSGeo4W\bin\` to `C:\OSGeo4W\apps\qgis\bin\` (adjust the paths if necessary).

Installing QGIS on Ubuntu

On Ubuntu, the QGIS project provides packages for both the release and developer versions. At the time of writing this book, the Ubuntu versions Precise, Saucy, and Trusty, are supported, but you can find the latest information at `http://qgis.org/en/site/forusers/alldownloads.html#ubuntu`. Be aware, though, that you can only install one version at a time. The packages are not listed in the default Ubuntu repositories. Therefore, we have to add the appropriate repositories to Ubuntu's source list, which you can find at `/etc/apt/sources.list`. You can open the file with any text editor.

Make sure that you have superuser rights, as you need them to save your edits. One option is to use `gedit`, which is installed on Ubuntu by default. To edit the `sources.list` file, use the following command:

```
sudo gedit /etc/apt/sources.list
```

Make sure that you add only one of the following four package-source options to avoid conflicts due to incompatible packages. The specific lines that you have to add to the source list depend on your Ubuntu version.

1. The first option, which is also the default one, is to install the current version. To install the QGIS release on Trusty Tahr, add the following lines to your file:

   ```
   deb     http://qgis.org/debian trusty main
   deb-src http://qgis.org/debian trusty main
   ```

   If necessary, replace `trusty` with `saucy` or `precise` to fit your system. For an updated list of supported Ubuntu versions, visit `http://download.qgis.org`.

2. The second option is to install the QGIS master, which is currently available for `trusty`, `saucy`, `utopic`, and `precise`. Add the following lines to your file:

   ```
   deb     http://qgis.org/debian-nightly trusty main
   deb-src http://qgis.org/debian-nightly trusty main
   ```

> The preceding versions depend on other packages such as `GDAL` and `proj4`, which are available in the Ubuntu repositories. It is worth mentioning that these packages are often quite old.

3. The third option is to install the QGIS release version with updated dependencies, which are provided by the `ubuntugis` repository. Add the following lines to your file:

   ```
   deb http://ppa.launchpad.net/ubuntugis/ubuntugis-unstable/ubuntu
   trusty main
   deb-src http://ppa.launchpad.net/ubuntugis/ubuntugis-unstable/
   ubuntu trusty main
   ```

4. The fourth option is the QGIS master with updated dependencies. Add the following lines to your file:

   ```
   deb     http://qgis.org/ubuntugis-nightly trusty main
   deb-src http://qgis.org/ubuntugis-nightly trusty main
   deb     http://ppa.launchpad.net/ubuntugis/ubuntugis-unstable/
   ubuntu trusty main
   ```

After choosing the repository, we will add the `qgis.org` repository's public key to our `apt` keyring. This will avoid warnings that you might otherwise get when installing from a non-default repository. Run the following command in the terminal:

```
gpg --keyserver keyserver.ubuntu.com --recv DD45F6C3
gpg --export --armor DD45F6C3 | sudo apt-key add -
```

> By the time this book goes into print, the key information might change. Refer to `http://qgis.org/en/site/forusers/alldownloads.html#ubuntu` for the latest updates.

Finally, to install QGIS, run the following commands:

```
sudo apt-get update
sudo apt-get install qgis python-qgis qgis-plugin-grass
```

Running QGIS for the first time

When you install QGIS, you get two applications: **QGIS Desktop** and **QGIS Browser**. If you are familiar with ArcGIS, you can think of QGIS Browser as similar to ArcCatalog. It is a small application to preview spatial data and related metadata. For the remainder of this book, we will focus on QGIS Desktop.

By default, QGIS uses the operating system's default language. To follow the tutorials in this book, I advise you to change the language to English by going to **Settings | Options | Locale**. On the first run, the way the toolbars are arranged can hide some buttons. To be able to work efficiently, I suggest that you rearrange the toolbars. I like to add some toolbars on the left and right screen borders to save vertical screen estate—especially on wide screen displays.

Additionally, we activate the file browser by going to **View** | **Panels** | **Browser**. It provides us with a quick access to our spatial data. In the end, the QGIS window on your screen should look similar to the following screenshot:

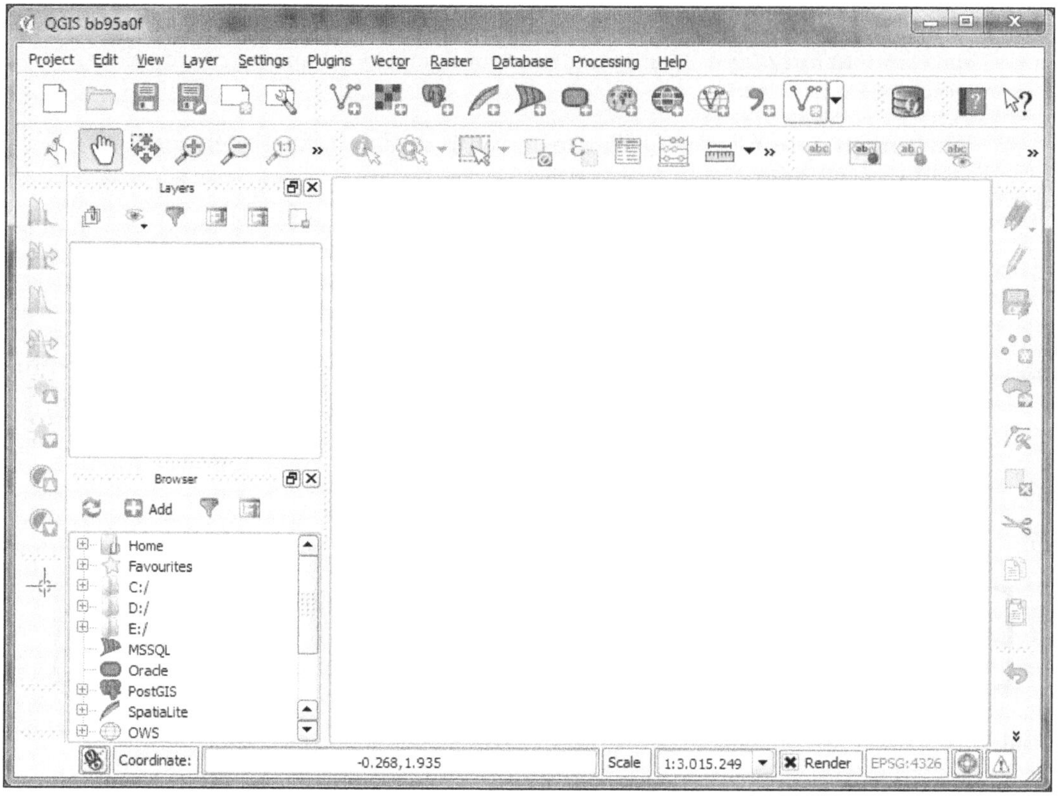

Next, we activate some must-have plugins by going to **Plugins** | **Manage and Install Plugins**. Plugins are activated by ticking the checkboxes beside their names. To begin with, I recommend the following:

- **Coordinate Capture**: This plugin is useful to pick coordinates in the map
- **fTools**: This plugin offers vector analysis and management tools
- **GdalTools**: This plugin offers raster analysis and management tools
- **Processing**: This plugin provides access to many useful raster and vector analyses tools as well as a model builder for task automation

To make it easier to find specific plugins, we can filter the list of plugins using the **Search** input field at the top of the window, which you can see in the following screenshot:

Introducing the QGIS user interface

Now that we have set up QGIS, let's get accustomed to the interface! As we already saw in the screenshot presented in the *Running QGIS for the first time* section, the biggest area is reserved for the map. To the left of the map, there are the **Layers** and **Browser** panels. In the following screenshot, you can see how the **Layers** panel looks like once we have loaded some layers (which we will do in the upcoming chapter *Viewing Spatial Data*). To the left of each layer entry, you can see a preview of the layer style. Additionally, we can use **layer groups** to structure the layer list. The **Browser** panel (shown in the following screenshot) provides us with a quick access to our spatial data, as you will soon see in the following chapter.

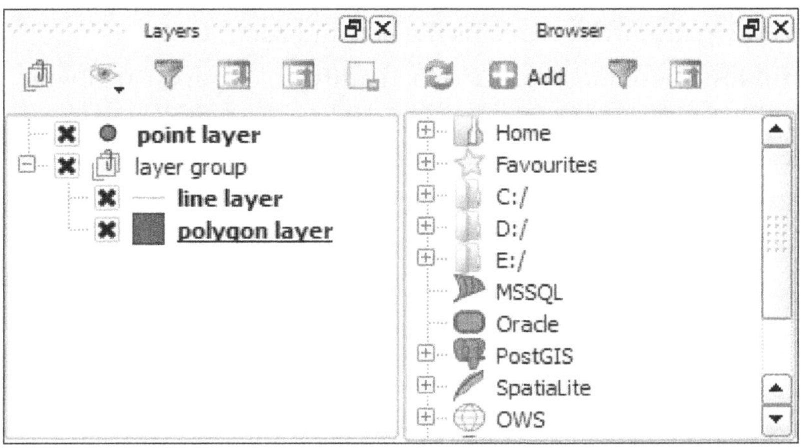

Below the map, we find important information such as (from left to right) the current map **Coordinates**, map **Scale**, and the (currently inactive) project **coordinate reference system** (**CRS**), for example, **EPSG:4326** in the following screenshot:

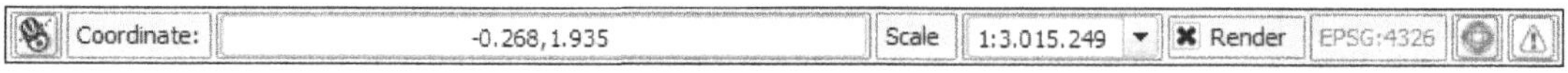

Next, there are multiple toolbars to explore. If you arrange them as shown in the previous section, the top row will look like this:

The first row contains the following toolbars:

- **File**: This toolbar contains the tools to create, open, save, and print projects
- **Manage Layers**: This toolbar contains the tools to add layers from the vector or raster files, databases, web services, and text files or create new layers
- **Database**: Currently, this toolbar only contains DB Manager, but other database-related tools (for example, the **OfflineEditing** plugin, which allows us to edit offline and synchronize with databases) will appear here when they are installed
- **Help**: Toolbar points to the option to download the user manual

The second row of toolbars looks like this:

The second row contains the following toolbars:

- **Map Navigation**: This contains the pan and zoom tools
- **Attributes**: These tools are used to identify, select, open attribute tables, measure, and so on
- **Label**: These tools are used to add, configure, and modify labels

On the left screen border, we will add the following toolbar:

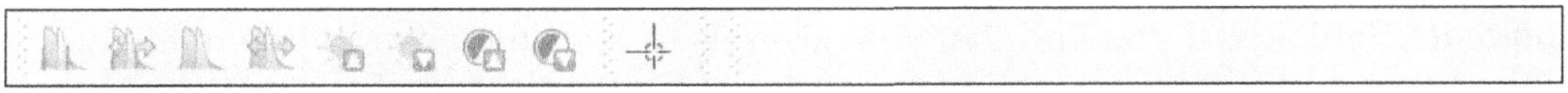

- **Raster**: This toolbar includes histogram stretch, brightness, and contrast control
- **Vector**: This currently only contains the **Coordinate Capture** tool, but it will be filled by additional Python plugins
- **Plugins**: This is currently empty, but will be filled by additional Python plugins
- **Web**: This is currently empty, but will be filled by additional Python plugins

Finally, on the right screen border, we find the following toolbar:

- **Digitizing**: The tools in this toolbar enable editing, basic feature creation, and editing
- **Advanced Digitizing**: This toolbar contains the undo/redo option, advanced editing tools, the geometry-simplification tool, and so on

> All digitizing tools are currently inactive. They will only turn active once we start editing a vector layer.

Toolbars and panels can be activated and deactivated via the **View** menu's **Panels** and **Toolbars** entries as well as by right-clicking on a menu or toolbar, which will open a context menu with all the available toolbars and panels. All the tools on the toolbars can also be accessed via the menu. If you deactivate the **Manage Layers** toolbar, for example, you will still be able to add layers using the **Layer** menu.

QGIS is highly customizable. You can increase your productivity by assigning shortcuts to the tools you use regularly, by navigating to **Settings** | **Configure shortcuts**. Similarly, if you find that you never use a certain toolbar button or menu entry, you can hide it by navigating to **Settings** | **Customization**. For example, if you don't have access to an Oracle Spatial database, you might want to hide the associated buttons to remove the clutter and save the screen estate, as shown in the following screenshot:

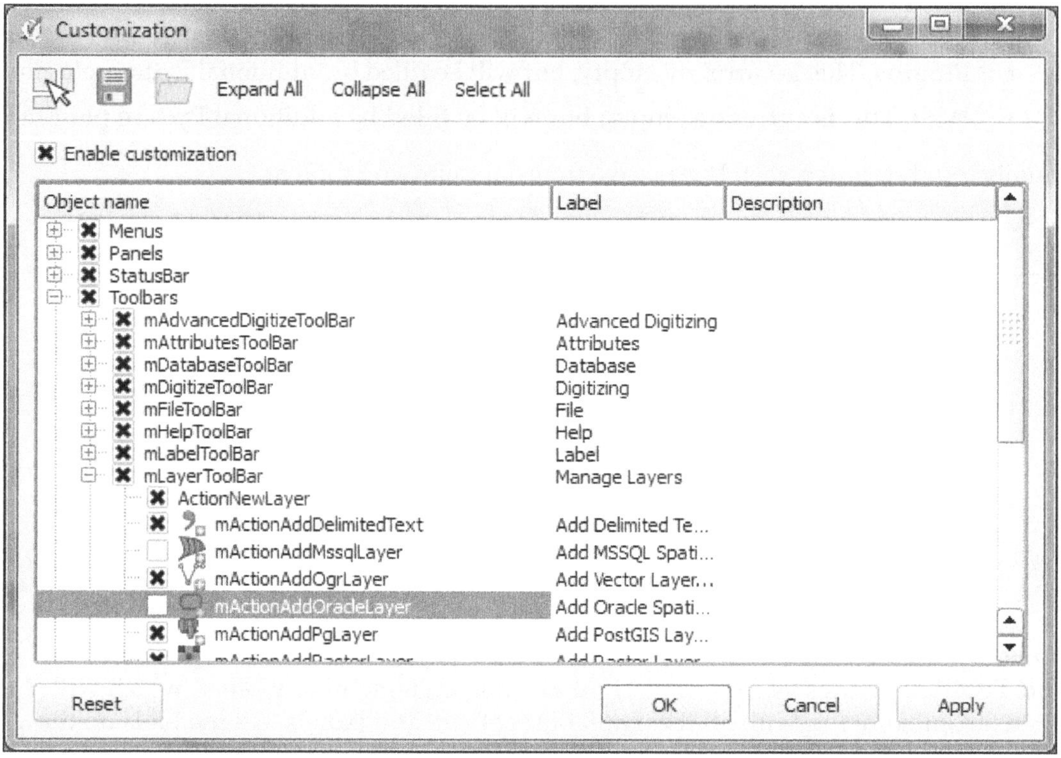

Summary

In this chapter, we installed QGIS and configured it by selecting useful defaults and arranging the user-interface elements. Finally, we explored the panels, toolbars, and menus that make up the QGIS user interface and learned how to customize them to increase productivity. In the following chapter, we will use QGIS to view spatial data from different data sources such as files, databases, and web services.

2
Viewing Spatial Data

In this chapter, we will cover how to view spatial data from different data sources. QGIS supports many file and database formats as well as standardized **OGC** (**Open Geospatial Consortium**) Web Services. We will first see how we can load layers from these different data sources. We will then look into the basics of styling both vector and raster layers and will create our first map, which you can see in the following screenshot:

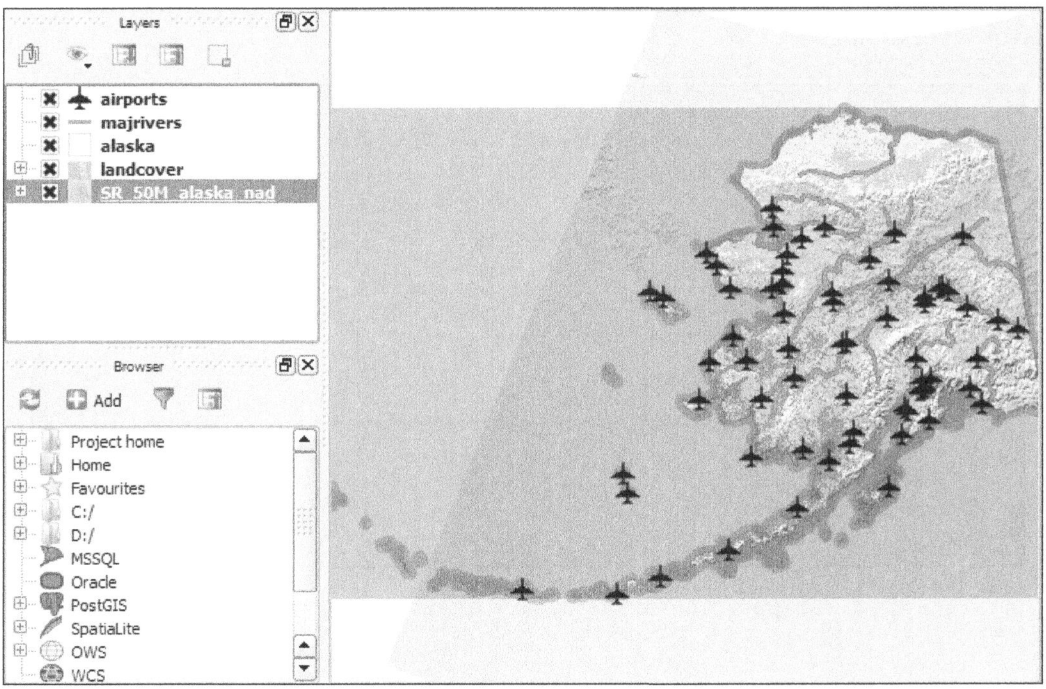

We will finish this chapter with an example of loading background maps from online services.

> For the examples in this chapter, we will use the sample data provided by the QGIS project, which is available for download from `download.osgeo.org/qgis/data/qgis_sample_data.zip` (21 MB). Download and unzip it.

Loading vector data from files

In this section, we will talk about loading vector data from GIS file formats, such as **Shapefiles**, as well as from text files.

We can load vector files by navigating to **Layer** | **Add vector layer** and also using the **Add vector layer** toolbar button. If you like shortcuts, use *Ctrl* + *Shift* + *V*. In the **Add vector layer** dialog, we will find a drop-down list that allows us to specify the encoding of the input file. This option is important if we are dealing with files that contain special characters, such as German umlauts or letters from alphabets different from the default Latin ones. The following screenshot shows the **Add vector layer** dialog:

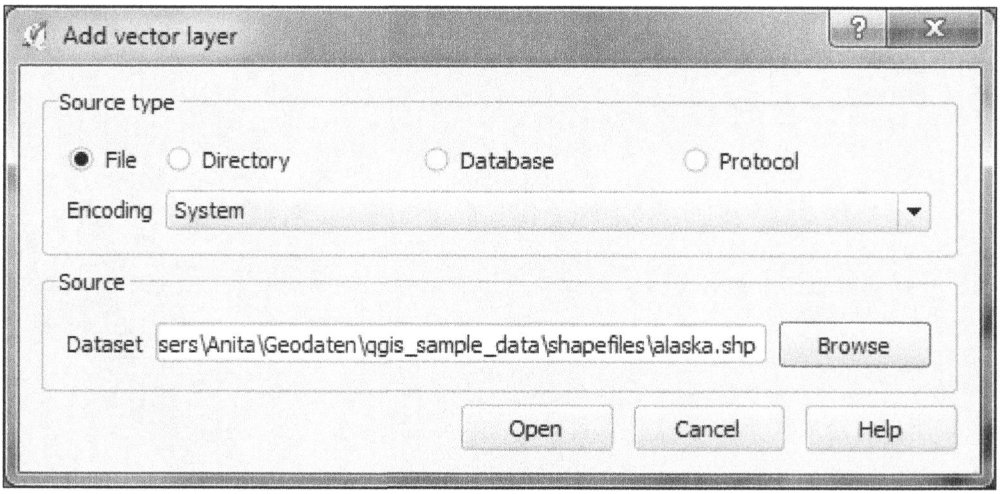

What we are most interested in now is the **Browse** button, which opens the file-opening dialog. Note the **file type filter** drop-down list in the bottom-right corner of the dialog. We can open it to see the list of the supported vector-file types. This filter is useful to find specific files faster by hiding all the files of a different type, but be aware that the filter settings are stored and will be applied again the next time we open the file-opening dialog.

This can be a source of confusion if we try to find a different file later and it happens to be hidden by the filter, so remember to check the filter settings if you are having trouble locating a file.

We can load more than one file in one go by selecting multiple files at once (holding down *Ctrl* on Windows/Ubuntu or *Cmd* on Mac). Let's give it a try.

1. First, we select `alaska.shp` and `airports.shp` from the `shapefiles` sample data folder.
2. Next, we confirm our selection by clicking on **Open**, and we are taken back to the **Add vector layer** dialog box.
3. After clicking on **Open** once more, the selected files are loaded. You will notice that each vector layer is displayed in a random color, which is most likely different from the color you see in the following screenshot. Don't worry about this now. We'll deal with layer styles later in this chapter.

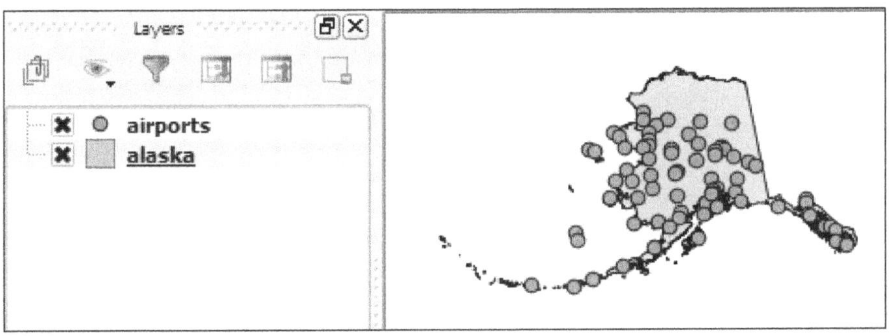

Even without using any spatial-analysis tools, these simple steps of visualizing spatial datasets enable us to find, for example, the southernmost airport on the Alaskan main land.

> There are multiple tricks that make loading data even faster; for example, you can simply drag-and-drop files from the operating system's file browser into QGIS.
>
> Another way to quickly access your spatial data is using QGIS's built-in file **browser**. If you set up QGIS as shown in *Chapter 1, Getting Started with QGIS*, you'll find the browser on the left-hand side, just below the layer list. Navigate to your data folder, and you can again drag-and-drop files from the browser to the map.
>
> Additionally, you can mark a folder as **favorite** by right-clicking on the folder and selecting **Add to favorites**. This way, you can access your data folders even faster, because they are added in the **Favorites** section right at the top of the browser list.

Another popular source of spatial data are **delimited text (CSV) files**. QGIS can load CSV files using the **Add Delimited Text Layer** option available via the menu entry by going to **Layers | Add Delimited Text Layer** or the corresponding toolbar button. Click on **Browse** and select `elevp.csv` from the sample data. CSV files come with all kinds of delimiters. As you can see in the following screenshot, the plugin lets you choose from the most common ones (**Comma**, **Tab**, and so on), but you can also specify any other plain or regular expression delimiter:

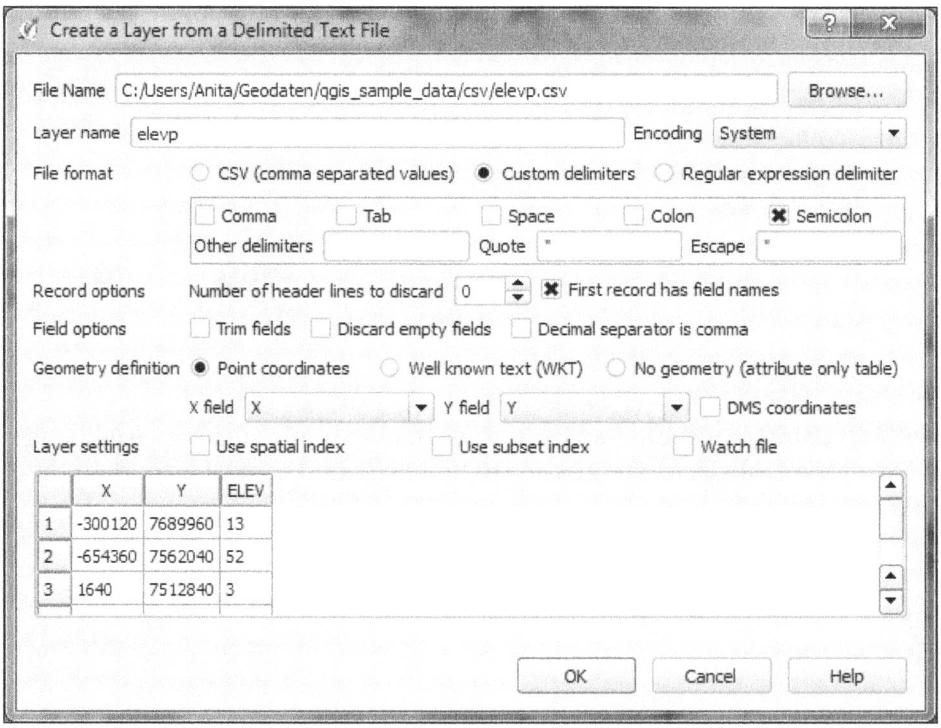

If your CSV file contains quotation marks such as `"` or `'`, you can use the **Quote** option to have them removed. The **Number of header lines to discard** option allows us to skip the extra lines at the beginning of the text file. The following **field options** include the functionality to trim extra spaces from field values or redefine the decimal separator to a comma. The spatial information itself can be provided either in two columns that contain the coordinates of points X and Y or using the **Well known text (WKT)** format. A WKT field can contain points, lines, or polygons.

> WKT is a very useful and flexible format. For example, a line can be specified by writing `LINESTRING (30 10, 10 30, 40 40)`. If you are unfamiliar with the concept, you can find an introduction with examples at `en.wikipedia.org/wiki/Well-known_text`.

After clicking on **OK**, QGIS will prompt us to specify the layer's **coordinate reference system** (**CRS**). We will talk about handling CRS next.

Dealing with coordinate reference systems

Whenever we load a data source, QGIS looks for usable CRS information, for example, in the Shapefile's `.prj` file. If QGIS cannot find any usable information, it will, by default, ask you to specify the CRS manually. This behavior can be changed by going to **Settings** | **Options** | **CRS** to always use either the project CRS or a default CRS.

The QGIS **Coordinate Reference System Selector** offers a filter that makes finding the CRS easier. It can filter by name or ID (for example, the EPSG code). Just start typing and watch how the list of potential CRSes gets shorter. There are actually two separate lists: the upper one contains the CRSes that we recently used, while the lower list is much longer and contains all the available CRSes. For the `elevp.csv` file, we will select **NAD27 / Alaska Albers**.

If we want to check a layer's CRS, we can find this information in the layer properties' **General** section, which can be accessed by going to **Layer** | **Properties** or by double-clicking on the layer name in the layer list. If you think that QGIS picked the wrong CRS or you made a mistake in specifying the CRS, you can correct the CRS settings using **Specify CRS**. Note that this does not change the underlying data or reproject it. We'll talk about reprojecting vectors and raster files in *Chapter 3, Data Creation and Editing*.

In QGIS, we can create a map out of multiple layers even if each dataset is stored with a different CRS. QGIS handles the necessary reprojections automatically by enabling a mechanism called **on-the-fly reprojection**, which can be accessed by going to **Project** | **Project Properties**, as seen in the following screenshot.

Alternatively, you can click on the **CRS status** button (with the globe symbol) in the bottom-right corner of the QGIS window to open this dialog.

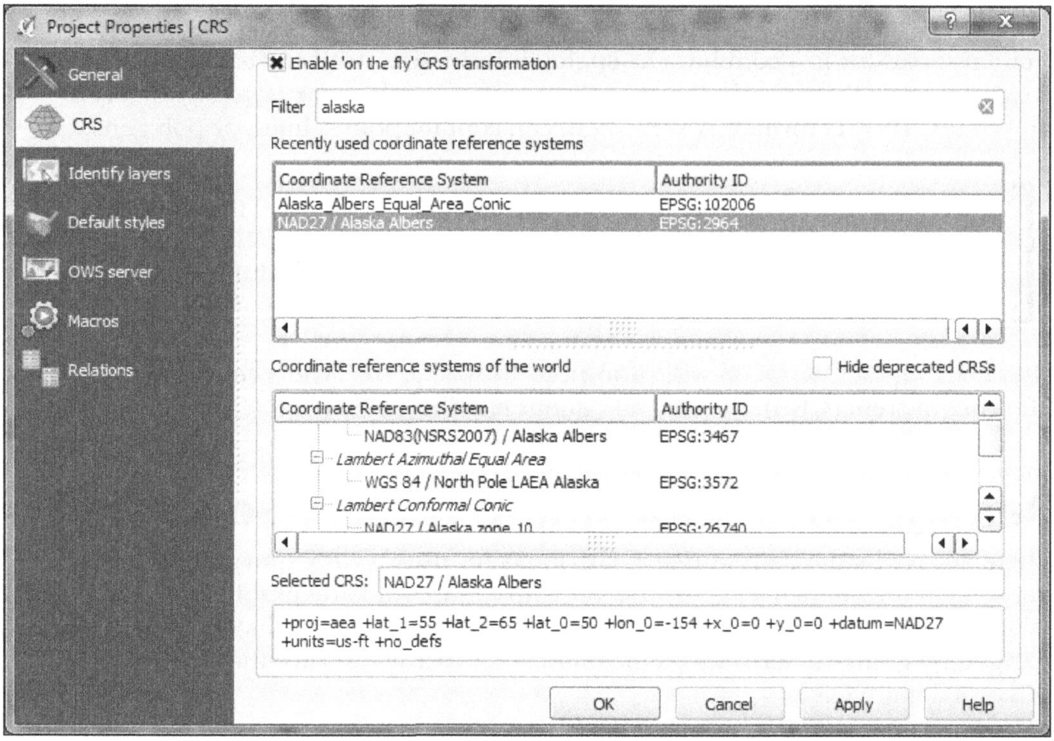

All layers are reprojected to the project CRS on the fly, which means that QGIS calculates these reprojections dynamically and only for the purpose of rendering the map. This also means that it can slow down your machine if you are working with big datasets that have to be reprojected. The underlying data is not changed and spatial analyses are not affected.

In some cases, you might have to specify a CRS that is not available in QGIS's CRS database. You can add CRS definitions by going to **Settings** | **Custom CRS**. Click on the **Add new CRS** button to create a new entry, type in a name for the new CRS, and paste the `proj4` definition string. This definition string is used by the **Proj4** projection engine to determine the correct coordinate transformation. Just close the dialog by clicking on **OK** when you are done.

> If you are looking for a specific projection `proj4` definition, `http://spatialreference.org` is a good source for this kind of information.

Loading raster files

Loading raster files is not much different to loading vector files. Selecting the **Layer** menu entry and then clicking on **Add Raster Layer**, clicking on the **Add Raster Layer** button, or pressing the *Ctrl* + *Shift* + *R* shortcut will take you directly to the file-opening dialog. Again, you can check the file type filter to see a list of the supported file types.

Let's give it a try and load `landcover.img` from the `raster` sample data folder. Similarly, just like vector files, you can load rasters by dragging them into QGIS from the operating system or the built-in file browser.

> Support for all these different vector and raster file types in QGIS is handled by the powerful `GDAL/OGR` package. You can check the full list of supported formats at `www.gdal.org/formats_list.html` (for rasters) and `www.gdal.org/ogr/ogr_formats.html` (for vectors).

Georeferencing raster maps

Some raster data sources, such as simple scanned maps, lack proper spatial referencing, and we have to georeference them before we can use them in a GIS. In QGIS, we can georeference rasters using the **Georeferencer** GDAL plugin, which can be accessed by going to **Raster** | **Georeferencer** (enable it by going to **Plugins** | **Manage and Install Plugins** if you cannot find it in the **Raster** menu).

The Georeferencer plugin covers the following use cases:

- We can create a world file for a raster file without altering the original raster.
- If we have a map image that contains points with known coordinates, we can set **ground control points** (**GCPs**) and enter the known coordinates.
- Finally, if we don't know the coordinates of any points on the map, we still have the chance to place GCPs manually using a second, already georeferenced map of the same area. We can use objects that are visible in both maps to pick points in the map that we want to georeference and work out their coordinates from the reference map.

After loading a raster in Georeferencer by going to **File** | **Open raster** or using the **Open raster** toolbar button, we are asked to specify the CRS of the ground-control points we are planning to add. Next, we can start adding ground-control points by going to **Edit** | **Add point**. We can use the pan and zoom tools to navigate, and we can place GCPs by clicking on the map. We are then prompted to insert the coordinates of the new point or pick them from the reference map in the main QGIS window. The placed GCPs are displayed as red circles in both the **Georeferencer** and the QGIS window, as you can see in the following screenshot:

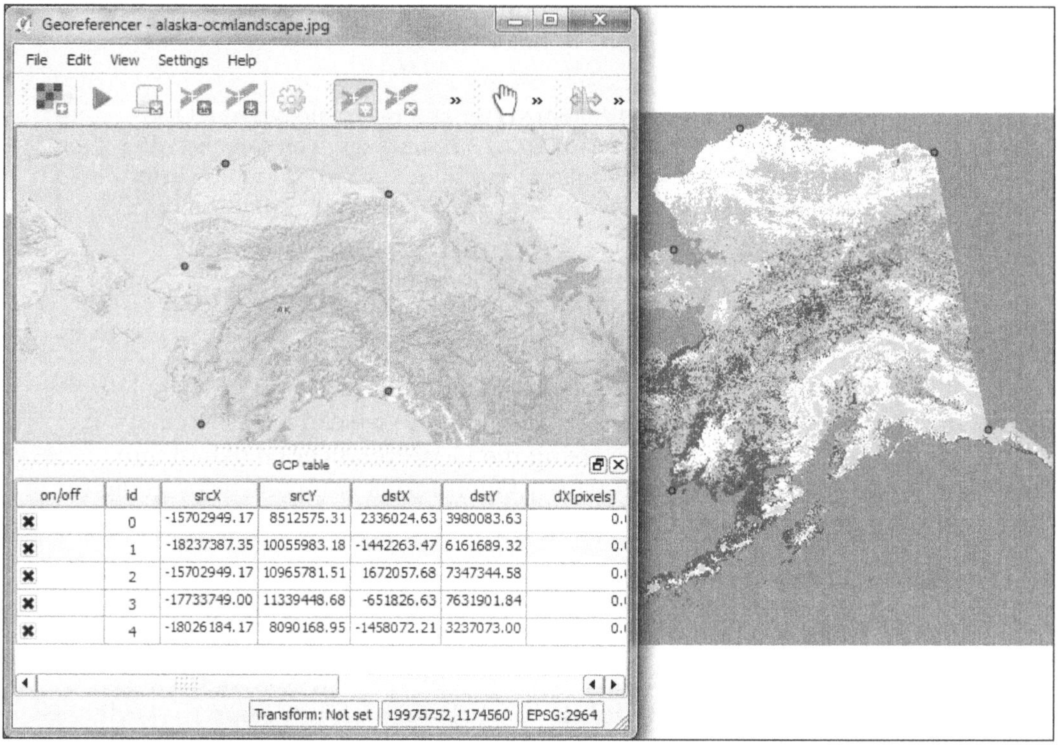

Georeferencer shows a screenshot of the OCM Landscape map Thunderforest, Data OpenStreetMap contributors (http://www.opencyclemap.org/?zoom=4&lat=61.39756&lon=-155.34668&layers=00B00)

After placing the GCPs, we can define the transformation algorithm by going to **Settings | Transformation Settings**. Which algorithm you choose depends on your input data and the level of geometric distortion you want to allow. The most commonly used algorithms are polynomials 1 to 3. A **first-order polynomial transformation** allows scaling, translation, and rotation only.

A **second-order polynomial transformation** can handle some curvature, and a **third-order polynomial transformation** consequently allows for even higher degrees of distortion. The **thin-plate spline** algorithm can handle local deformations in the map and is therefore very useful when working with very low-quality map scans. The **projective** transformation offers rotation and translation of coordinates. The **linear** option, on the other hand, is only used to create world files, and as mentioned earlier, this does not actually transform the raster.

The **resampling method** depends on your input data and the result you want to achieve. Cubic resampling creates smooth results, but if you don't want to change the raster values, choose the nearest neighbor method.

Before we can start the georeferencing process, we have to specify the output filename and target CRS. Make sure that the **Load in QGIS when done** option is active and activate the **Use 0 for transparency when needed** option to avoid black borders around the output image. Then, we can close the **Transformation Settings** dialog and go to **File | Start Georeferencing**. The georeferenced raster will automatically be loaded into the main map window of QGIS. In the following screenshot, you can see the result of applying a projective transformation using the five specified GCPs:

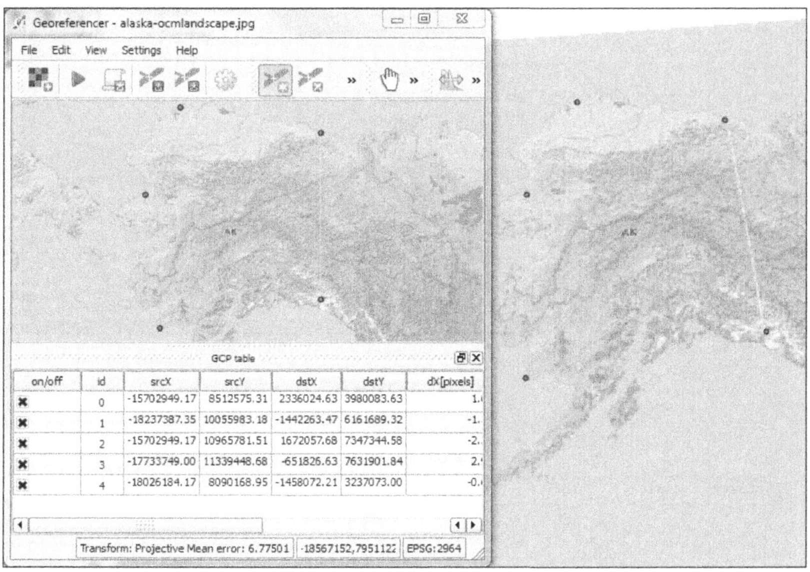

Loading data from databases

QGIS supports PostGIS, SpatiaLite, MSSQL, SQL Anywhere, and Oracle Spatial databases. We will cover two open source options: SpatiaLite and PostGIS. Both are available cross platform, just like QGIS.

SpatiaLite is the spatial extension for SQLite databases. SQLite is a self-contained, serverless, zero-configuration, and transactional SQL database engine (`www.sqlite.org`). This basically means that a SQLite database, and therefore, also a SpatiaLite database, doesn't need a server installation and can be copied and exchanged just like any ordinary file.

You can download an example database from `www.gaia-gis.it/spatialite-2.3.1/test-2.3.zip` (4 MB). Unzip the file; you will be able to connect to it by going to **Layer** | **Add SpatiaLite Layer**, using the **Add SpatiaLite Layer** toolbar button, or by pressing *Ctrl* + *Shift* + *L*. Click on **New** to select the `test-2.3.sqlite` database file. QGIS will save all connections and add them to the drop-down list at the top. After clicking on **Connect**, you will see the list of layers stored in the database, as shown in the following screenshot:

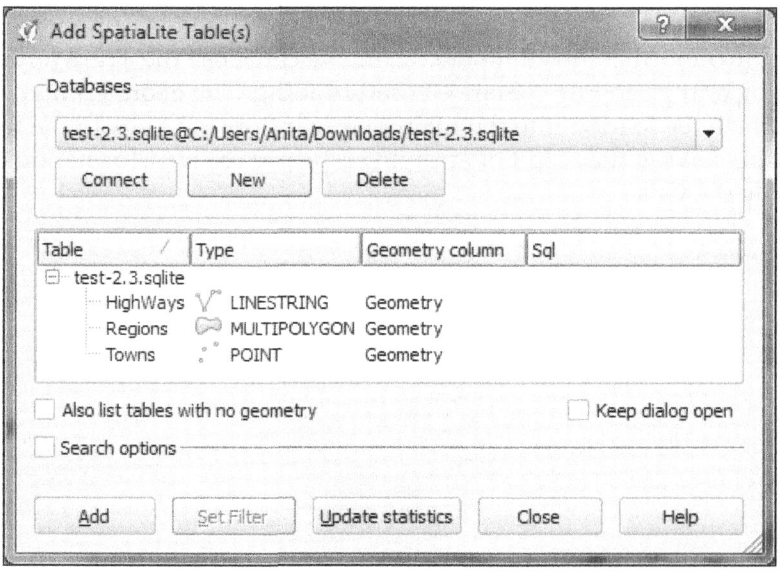

Like with files, you can select one or more tables from the list and click on **Add** to load them into the map. Additionally, you can use **Set Filter** to load only specific features.

> Filters in QGIS use SQL-like syntax, for example, `"Name" = 'EMILIA-ROMAGNA'` to select only the region called `EMILIA-ROMAGNA` or `"Name" LIKE 'ISOLA%'` to select all the regions that start with `ISOLA`. The filter queries are passed on to the underlying data provider (for example, SpatiaLite or OGR). The provider syntax for basic filter queries is consistent over different providers but can vary when using more exotic functions. You can read up on the details of OGR SQL at `http://www.gdal.org/ogr/ogr_sql.html`.

PostGIS is the spatial extension for the PostgreSQL database system. Installing and configuring the database is out of the scope of this book, but there are installers for Windows and packages for many Linux distributions as well as for Mac. (For details, visit `http://www.postgresql.org/download/`. To load data from a PostGIS database, go **Layers** | **Add PostGIS Layer**, use the **Add PostGIS Layer** toolbar button, or press *Ctrl* + *Shift* + *D*.

When using a database for the first time, click on **New** to establish a new database connection. In the following dialog box, you can specify a name for the new connection. Other fields that have to be filled in are as follows:

- **Host**: The server's IP address is inserted in this field. You can use `localhost` if PostGIS is running locally.
- **Port**: The PostGIS default port is `5432`. If you have trouble reaching a database, it is recommended that you check the server's firewall settings for this port.
- **Database**: This is the name of the PostGIS database you want to connect to.
- **Username** and **Password**: For convenience, you can tell QGIS to save them.

The following screenshot shows the dialog to create a new connection to a database called `postgis`:

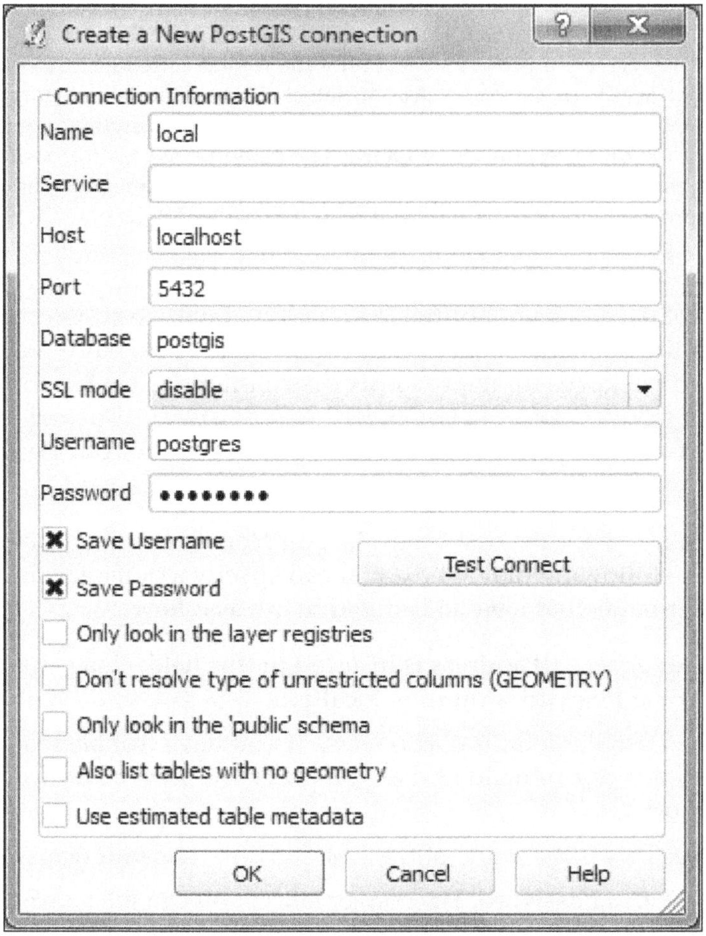

After the connection is established, you can load and filter tables, just like we discussed for SpatiaLite.

Loading data from OGC Web Services

More and more data providers offer access to their datasets via OGC-compliant web services such as WMS, WCS, or WFS. QGIS supports these services out of the box.

> If you want to learn more about the different OGC Web Services available, visit `http://live.osgeo.org/en/standards/standards.html` for an overview.

You can load WMS layers by going to **Layer** | **Add WMS/WMTS Layer**, by clicking on the **Add WMS/WMTS Layer** button, or by pressing *Ctrl* + *Shift* + *W*. If you know a WMS server, you can connect to it by clicking on **New** and filling in a name and the URL. All other fields are optional. Don't worry if you don't know of any WMS server, because we can simply click on **Add default servers** to get access information about servers whose administrators collaborate with the QGIS project. One of these servers is called **Lizardtech server**. Select **Lizardtech server**, or any of the other servers, from the drop-down box, and click on **Connect** to see the list of layers available through the server.

From the layer list, you can now select one or more layers for download. It is worth noting that the order in which you select the layers matters, because the layers will be combined on the server side, and QGIS will only receive the combined image as the resultant layer. If you want to be able to use the layers separately, you have to download them one by one. The data download starts once you click on **Add**. The dialog will stay open so that you can add additional layers from the server.

Many WMS servers offer their layers in multiple, different CRSes. You can check the list of available CRSes by clicking on the **Change** button at the bottom of the dialog. This will open a CRS selector dialog, which is limited to the WMS server's CRS capabilities.

Loading data from WCS or WFS servers works in the same way, but public servers are rare and unreliable and therefore, no recommendation can be provided here.

Styling raster layers

After this introduction to data sources, we can now create our first map. We will build the map from the bottom up by first loading some background rasters (hillshade and land cover), which we will then overlay with point, line, and polygon layers.

Let's start by loading land cover and hillshade from `landcover.img` and `SR_50M_alaska_nad.tif` and then opening the **Style** section in layer properties (by navigating to **Layer** | **Properties** or by double-clicking on the layer name). QGIS tries to pick a reasonable default render type. The following style options are available for raster layers:

- **Multiband color**: This style is used if the raster has several bands. This is usually the case with satellite images with multiple bands.
- **Paletted**: This style is used if a single band raster comes with an indexed palette.
- **Singleband gray**: If a raster has neither multiple bands nor an indexed palette (this is the case, for example, with elevation-model rasters or hillshade rasters), it will be rendered using the single band gray style.
- **Singleband pseudocolor**: Instead of being limited to gray, this style allows us to render a raster band using a color map of our choice.

The `SR_50M_alaska_nad.tif` hillshade raster is loaded with **Singleband gray Render type**, as you can see in the following screenshot. If we want to render the hillshade raster in color instead of grayscale, we can change **Render type** to **Singleband pseudocolor**. In the pseudocolor mode, we can create color maps either manually or by selecting one of the premade color ramps. However, let's stick to **Singleband gray** for hillshade for now.

Below the color settings, we will find a section with more advanced options that control raster resampling, brightness, contrast, saturation, and hue—options you probably know from image-processing software. By default, resampling is set to the fast **Nearest neighbour** option. To get nice smooth results, we can change to the **Bilinear** or **Cubic** method.

Click on **Ok** or **Apply** to confirm. In both cases, the map will be redrawn using the new layer style. If you click on **Apply**, the **Layer Properties** dialog stays open, and you can continue to fine-tune the layer style. If you click on **Ok**, the **Layer Properties** dialog will be closed.

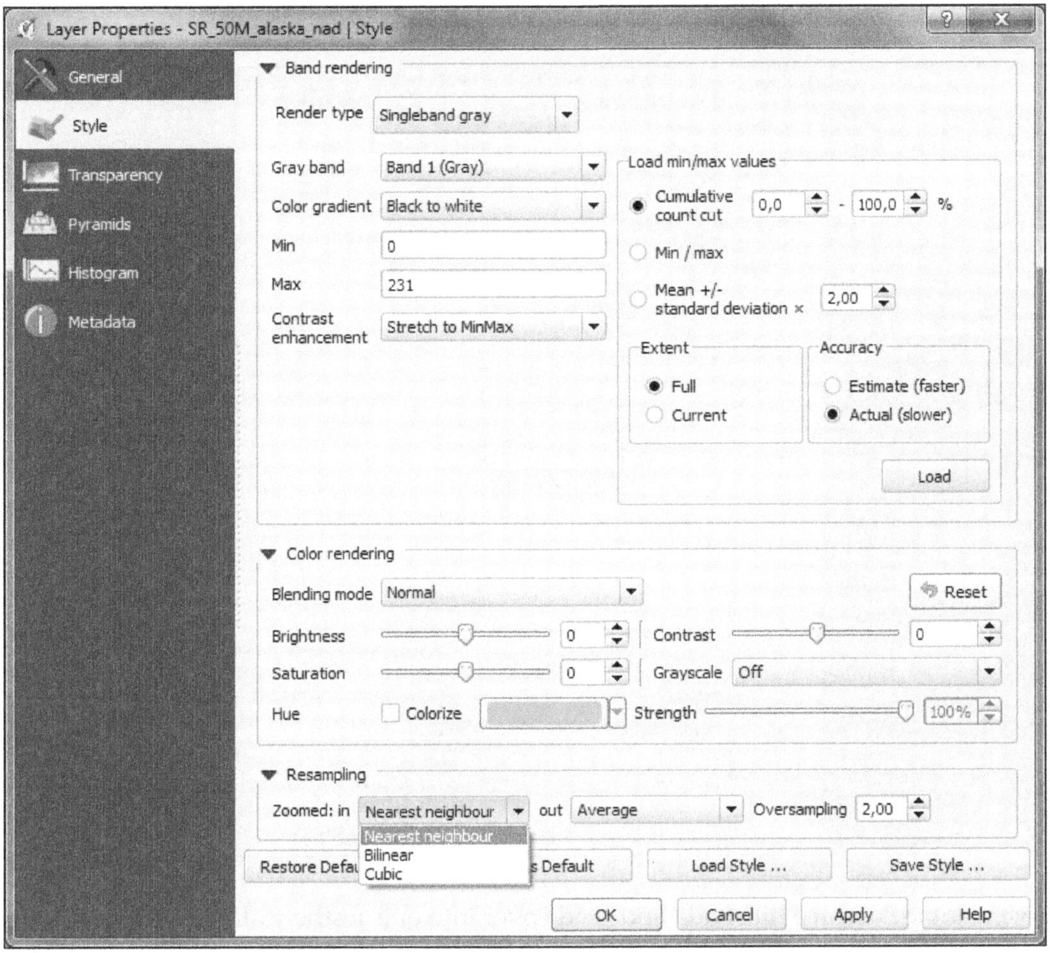

The `landcover.img` raster is a good example of a paletted raster. Each cell value is mapped to a specific color. To change a color, we can simply double-click on the **Color** preview, and a color picker will open.

The style section of a paletted raster looks like the following screenshot:

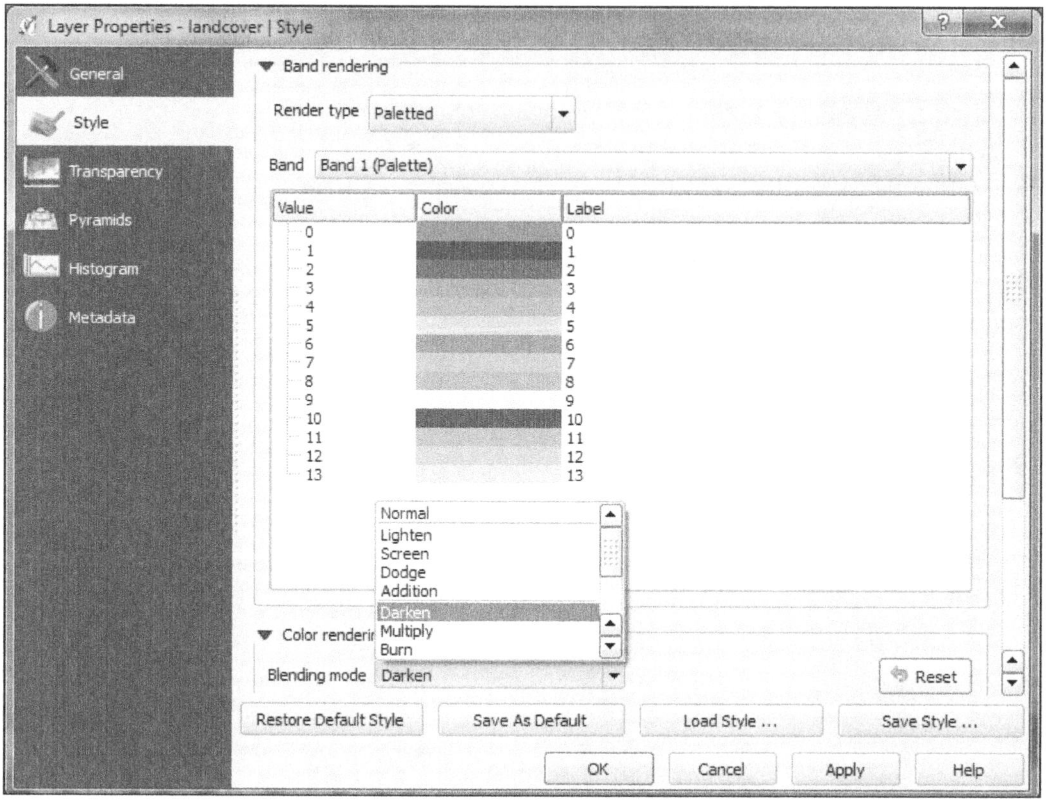

If we want to combine hillshade and land cover into one aesthetically-pleasing background, we can use a combination of the **Blending mode** and layer **Transparency**. Blending modes are another feature commonly found in image-processing software. The main advantage of blending modes over transparency is that we can avoid the usually dull, low-contrast look that results from combining rasters using transparency alone. If you haven't had any experience with blending, take some time to try the different effects. For this example, I used the **Darken** blending mode, as highlighted in the previous screenshot, together with a global layer transparency of **50%**, as shown in the following screenshot:

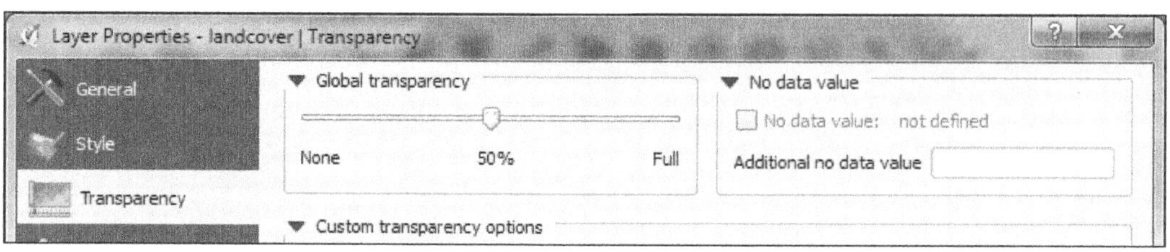

Styling vector layers

When we load vector layers, QGIS renders them using a default style and a random color. Of course, we want to customize these styles to better reflect our data. In the following exercises, we will style point, line, and polygon layers, and we will also get accustomed to the most common vector-styling options.

Regardless of the layer's geometry type, we will always find a drop-down list with the available style options in the upper-left corner of the **Style** dialog.

The following style options are available for vector layers:

- **Single Symbol**: This is the simplest option. When we use a **Single Symbol** style, all points are displayed with the same symbol.
- **Categorized**: This is the style of choice if a layer contains points of different categories, for example, a layer that contains locations of different animal sightings.
- **Graduated styles**: These are great if we want to visualize numerical values; for example, temperature measurements.
- **Rule-based styles**: This is the most advanced option. These styles are very flexible, because they allow us to write multiple rules for one layer.
- **Point displacement styles**: This is only available for point layers. These styles are useful if you need to visualize point layers with multiple points at the same coordinates, for example, students of a school living at the same address.
- **Inverted polygons**: Using this option, the defined symbology will be applied to the area outside the polygon borders instead of filling the area inside the polygon.

Creating point styles – an example of an airport style

Let's get started with a point layer! Load `airport.shp` from our sample data. In the upper-left corner of the **Style** dialog, below the drop-down list, we will find the symbol preview. Below this, there is the list of symbol layers that shows us the different layers that the symbol consists of. On the right-hand side, we will find options for the symbol size and size units, color and transparency, as well as rotation. Using the **Data defined properties** button, we can also tell QGIS to use the feature's attribute values to define symbol shape, size, color, and so on. Finally, the bottom-right area contains a preview area with saved symbols.

Point layers are, by default, displayed using a simple circle symbol. We want to use a symbol of an airplane instead. To change the symbol, select the **Simple marker** entry in the symbol layers list on the left-hand side of the dialog. Notice how the right-hand side of the dialog changes. We can now see the options available for simple markers: **Colors**, **Size**, **Rotation**, **Form**, and so on. However, we are not looking for circles, stars, or square symbols—we want an airplane. That's why we need to change the **Symbol layer type** option from **Simple marker** to **SVG marker**. Many of the options are similar, but at the bottom, we will now find a selection of SVG images that we can choose from. Scroll through the list and pick the airplane symbol, as shown in the following screenshot:

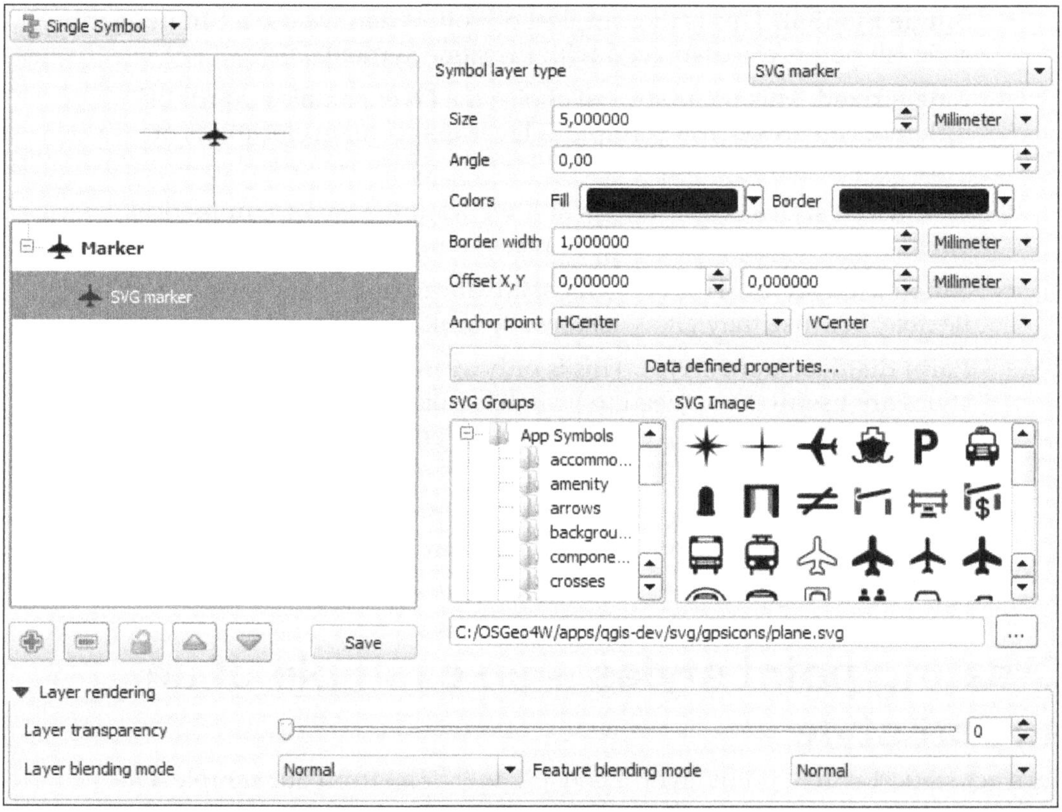

Symbol layer types for point layers include the following:

- **Simple marker**: This includes geometric forms such as circles, stars, and squares
- **Font marker**: This provides access to your symbol fonts
- **SVG marker**: Each QGIS installation comes with a collection of default SVG symbols; add your own folders that contain SVG images by going to **Settings** | **Options** | **System** | **SVG Paths**
- **Ellipse marker**: This includes customizable ellipses, rectangles, crosses, and triangles, which are especially useful when combined with what we set in the data-defined-settings option
- **Vector Field marker**: This is a customizable vector-field visualization tool

Creating line styles – an example of river or road styles

In this exercise, we will create a river style for the `majriver.shp` file in our sample data. The goal is to create a line style with two colors: a fill color for the center of the line and an outline color. This technique is very useful because it can also be used to create road styles.

To create such a style, we will combine two simple lines. The default symbol is one simple line. Click on the green + symbol located below the symbol layers list in the bottom-left corner to add another simple line. The lower line will be our outline, and the upper one will be the fill. Select the upper simple line and change the color to blue and the width to 0.3 millimeters. Next, select the lower simple line and change its color to gray and the width to 0.6 millimeters, slightly wider than the other line. Check the preview and click on **Apply** to test how the style looks when applied to the river layer.

You will notice that the style doesn't look perfect yet. This is because each line feature is drawn separately, one after the other, and this leads to a rather disconnected appearance. Luckily, this is easy to fix; we only need to enable the so-called symbol levels. To do this, select the **Line** entry in the symbol layers list and tick the checkbox in the **Symbol Levels** dialog of the **Advanced** section (the button in the lower-right corner of the style dialog), as shown in the following screenshot. Click on **Apply** to test the results.

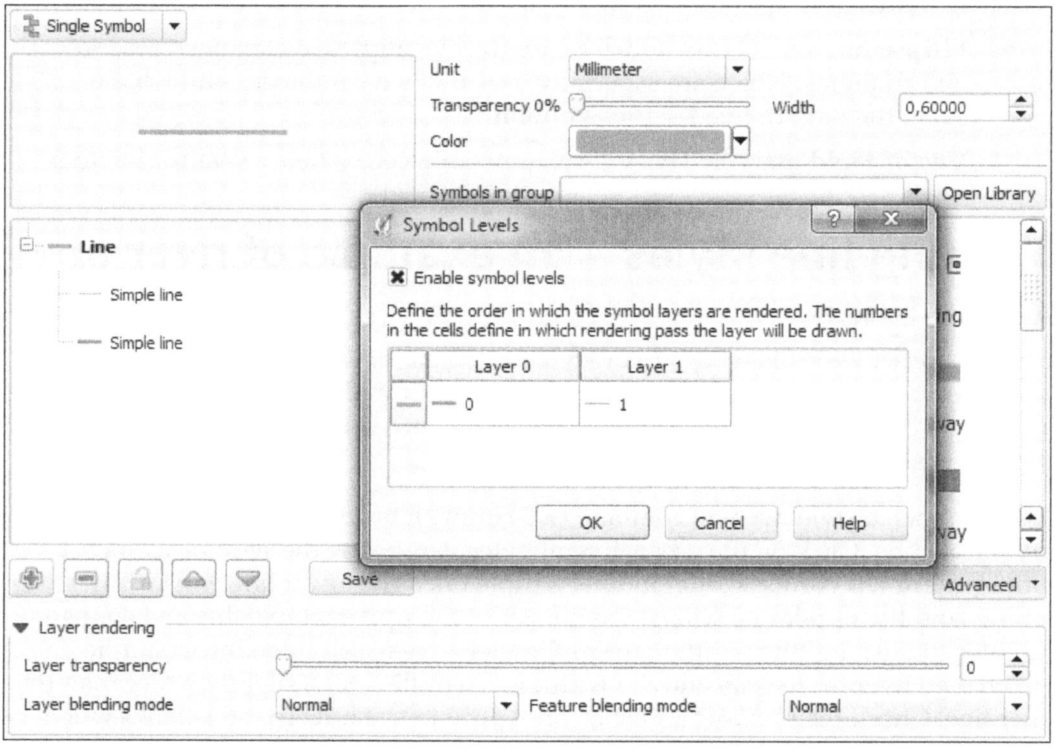

Symbol layer types for line layers include the following:

- **Simple line**: This is a solid or dashed line
- **Marker line**: This line is made out of point markers located at line vertices or at regular intervals

> Whenever we create a symbol that we might want to reuse in other maps, we can save it by clicking on the **Save** button under the symbol layers list. We can assign a name to the new symbol, and after we save it, it will be added to the saved symbols preview area on the right-hand side.

Creating polygon styles – an example of a landmass style

In this exercise, we will create a style for the `alaska.shp` file. The goal is to create a simple fill with a blue halo. Like in the previous river-style example, we will combine two symbol layers to create this style: a **Simple fill** layer that defines the main fill color (white) with a thin border (in gray) and an additional **Simple line** outline layer for the (light blue) halo. The halo should have nice rounded corners. To achieve these, change the **Join style** option of the **Simple line** symbol layer to **Round**. Similar to the previous example, we will again enable symbol levels; to prevent this landmass style from blocking out the background map, we will select the **Multiply** blending mode, as shown in the following screenshot:

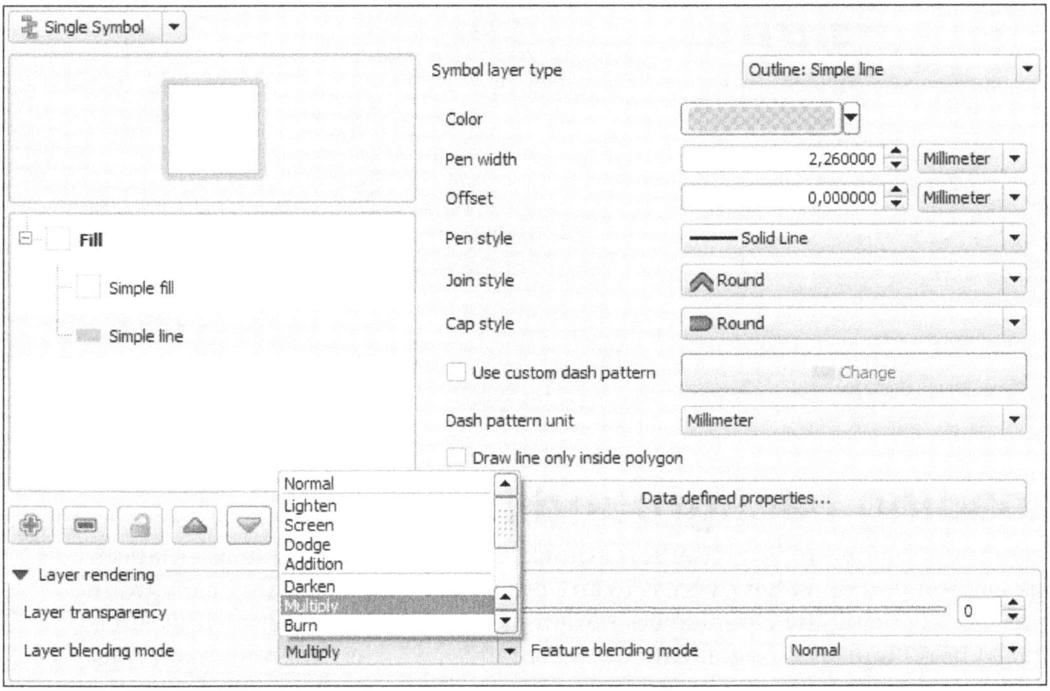

Symbol layer types for polygon layers include the following:

- **Simple fill**: This defines the fill and outline colors as well as the basic fill styles
- **Centroid fill**: This allows us to put point markers at the center of polygons
- **Line/Point pattern fill**: This supports user-defined lines and point patterns with flexible spacing

- **SVG fill**: This fills the polygon using SVG patterns
- **Gradient fill**: This allows us to fill polygons with linear, radial, or conical gradients
- **Shapeburst fill**: This is also known as a "buffered" gradient fill. It creates a gradient that starts at the polygon border and flows towards the center. The following screenshot shows a fixed-distance shading using the **Shade to a set distance** option. If we select **Shade whole shape** instead, the gradient will be drawn from the polygon border to the center.
- **Outline**: This makes it possible to outline areas using line styles

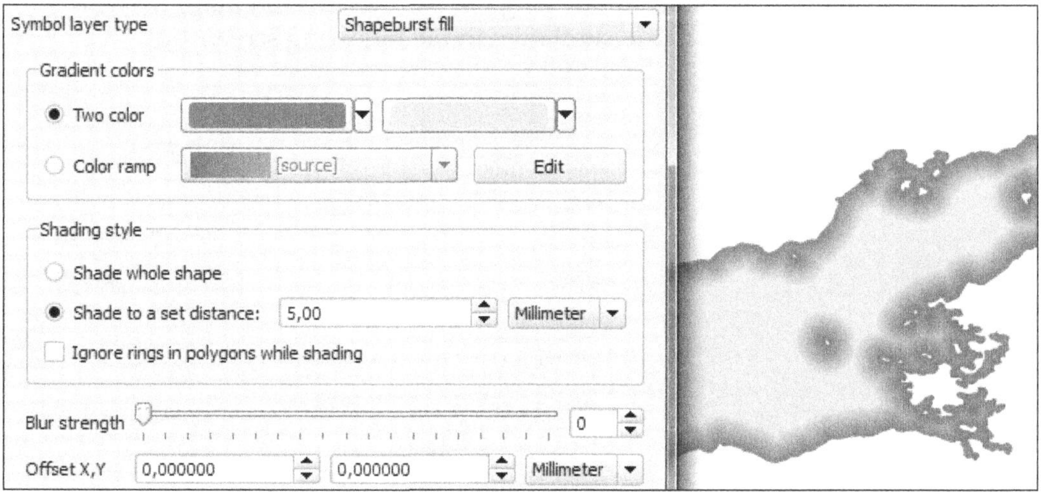

Loading background maps

Background maps are very useful for quick checks and to provide orientation, especially if you don't have access to any other base layers. Adding background maps is easy using the OpenLayers plugin. It provides access to satellite, street, and hybrid maps by Google, Yahoo!, and Bing, as well as different map types by OpenStreetMap, Stamen, and Apple.

To install the OpenLayers plugin, go to **Plugins | Manage and Install Plugins**. Wait until the list of available plugins has finished loading. Use the filter to look for the **OpenLayers Plugin** option, as shown in the following screenshot. Select it from the list and click on **Install plugin**. This is going to take a moment. Once it's done, you will see a short confirmation message. You can then close the installer, and the **OpenLayers Plugin** option will be available through the **Web** menu.

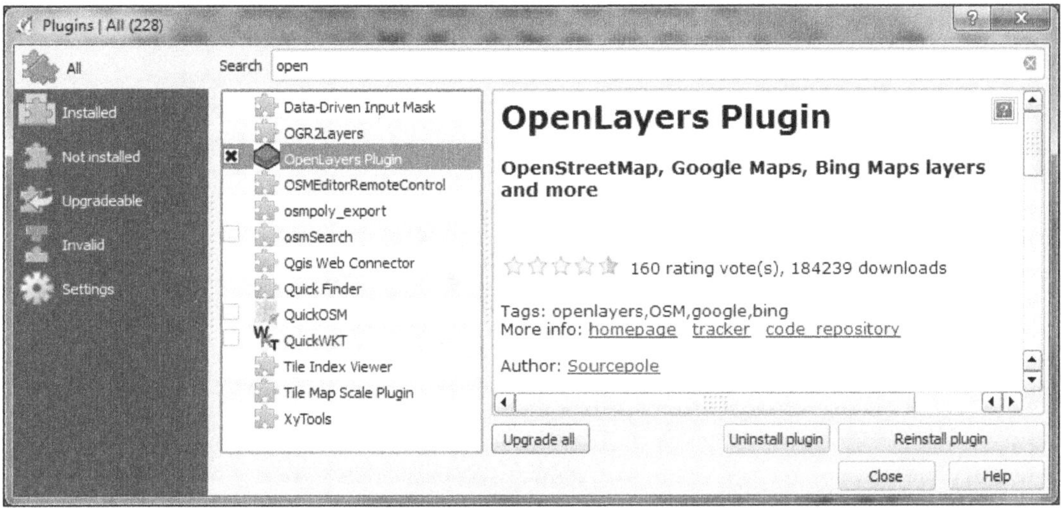

Note that you have to be online to use these services. Another fact worth mentioning is that all these services provide their maps only in Pseudo Mercator (EPSG:3857). Your project CRS will automatically be changed to Pseudo Mercator when you load a background map using the **OpenLayers plugin** option.

> Background maps added using **OpenLayers plugin** are not suitable for printing due to their low-resolution and alignment issues in **Print Composer**.

If you load the **OCM Landscape** layer, your map will look like the following screenshot:

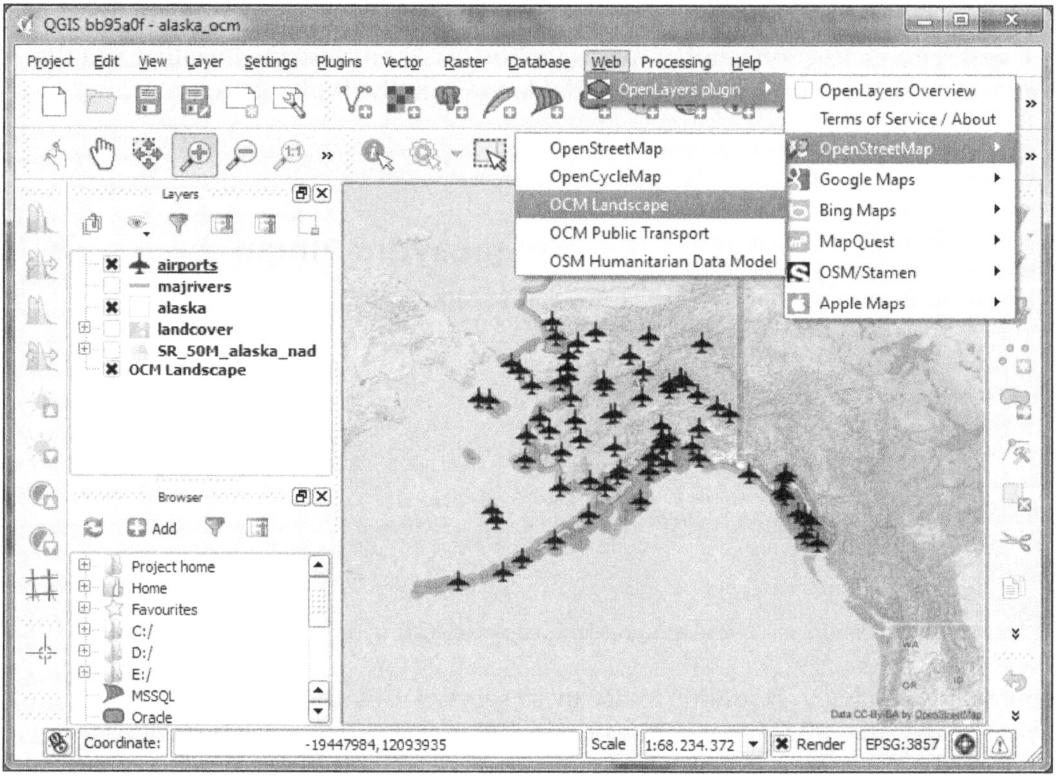

Summary

In this chapter, you learned how to load spatial data from files, databases, and web services. You saw how QGIS handles coordinate reference systems and had your first introduction to styling vector and raster layers, a topic we will cover in more detail in *Chapter 5, Creating Great Maps*. We also installed our first Python plugin, the OpenLayers plugin, and used it to load background maps into our project. In the following chapter, we will go into more detail and learn how to create and edit raster and vector data.

3

Data Creation and Editing

In this chapter, you will first create some new vector layers and learn how to select features and take measurements. We will then continue with editing feature geometries and attributes. Then, we will reproject vector and raster data, and before we end this chapter, you will learn how to convert between different file formats with joining data from text files and spreadsheets to our spatial data.

Creating new vector layers

In this exercise, we'll create a new layer from scratch. QGIS offers a wide range of functionalities to create different layers. The **New** menu under **Layer** lists the functions to create new Shapefile and SpatiaLite layers, but we can also create new database tables using the DB Manager plugin. The interfaces differ slightly to accommodate the features supported by each format.

Let's create a new shapefile to see how it works. A new Shapefile layer, which can be accessed by going to **Layer** | **New** or by pressing *Ctrl* + *Shift* + *N*, opens the **New Vector Layer** dialog with options for different geometry types, CRSes, and attributes. The process itself is really fast because all the mandatory fields already have default values. By default, it will create a new point layer with WGS84 CRS (unless specified otherwise by going to **Settings** | **Options** | **CRS**) and one integer field called **id**. We can simply click on **OK** and specify a filename. This creates a new Shapefile, and the new Shapefile layer appears in the layer list.

Next, we also create one line and one polygon layer. We'll add some extra fields to these layers. Besides integer fields, shapefiles also support text and decimal values. To add a field, we only need to insert a name, select a type and width, and click on **Add to attributes list**. For decimal numbers, we also have to define the **Precision** value, which determines the number of digits after the comma. A **Width** value of **3** with a **Precision** value of **1** will allow a value range from -99.9 to + 99.9. The following screenshot shows the **New Vector Layer** dialog and the **Attributes...** window for my example polygon layer:

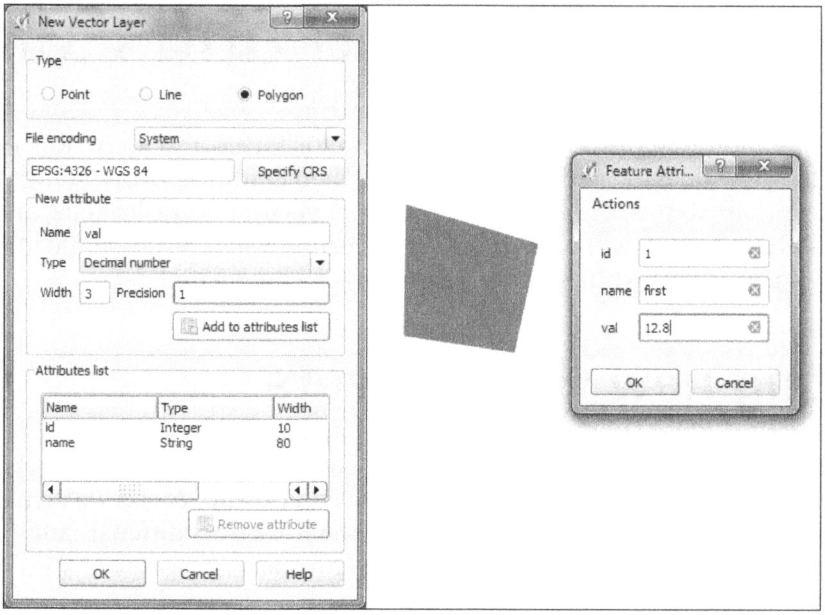

All of the new layers are empty so far, but we will create some features now. If we want to add features to a layer, we first have to enable editing for this layer. Editing can be turned on and off either by going to **Layer** | **Toggle editing** or **Toggle editing** in the layer name context menu or by clicking on the **Toggle editing** button in the **Digitizing** toolbar. You will notice that the layer's icon in the layer list changes to reflect whether editing is on or off. When we turn on editing for a layer, QGIS automatically enables the digitizing tools suitable for the layer's geometry type.

Now, we can use the **Add Feature** tool in the editing toolbar to create new features. To place a point, we can simply click on the map. We are then prompted to fill in the attribute form, which you can see on the right-hand side of the previous screenshot, and once we click on **OK**, the new feature is created. Like with points, we can create new lines and polygons by placing nodes on the map. To finish a line or polygon, we can simply right-click on the map. Create some features in each layer and then save your changes. We can reuse these test layers in the upcoming exercises.

New features and feature edits are saved permanently only after clicking on the **Save Layer Edits** button in the **Digitizing** toolbar or once we finish editing and confirm that we want to save them.

Working with feature selection tools

Selecting features is one of the core functions of any GIS, and it is useful to know them before we venture into editing geometries and attributes. Depending on the use case, selection tools come in many different flavors. QGIS offers three different kinds of tools to select features—using the mouse, an expression, or another layer.

The first group of tools in the **Attributes** toolbar allows us to select features on the map using the mouse. The following screenshot shows the **Select Feature(s)** tool. We can select a single feature by clicking on it or select multiple features by drawing a rectangle. The other tools can be used to select features by drawing different shapes—polygons, freehand areas, or circles—around the features. All features that intersect with the drawn shape are selected. Holding down the *Ctrl* key will add the new selection to an existing one. Similarly, holding down *Ctrl* + *Shift* will remove the new selection from the existing one.

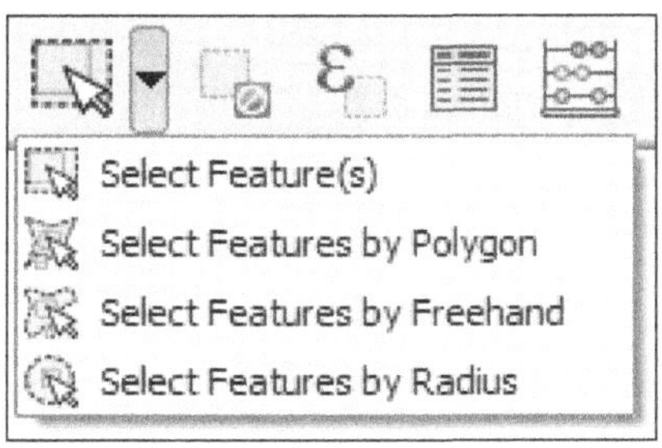

The second type of select tool is called **Select by Expression**, and it is also available in the **Attribute** toolbar. It selects features based on expressions that can contain references and functions using feature attributes and/or geometry. The list of available functions is pretty long, but we can use the search box to filter the list by name to find the function we are looking for faster. On the right-hand side of the window, we find **Selected Function Help**, which explains the functionality and how to use the function in an expression. The **Function List** shows the layer attribute fields, and by clicking on **Load all unique values** or **Load 10 sample values**, we can easily access their content. Like with the mouse tools, we can choose between creating a new selection or adding to or deleting from an existing selection. Additionally, we can choose to only select features from within an existing selection.

Let's have a look at some example expressions that you can build on and use in your own work:

- Using the `lakes.shp` file in our sample data, we can, for example, select big lakes with an area bigger than 1,000 square miles using a simple `"AREA_MI" > 1000.0` attribute query or using geometry functions such as `$area > (1000.0 * 27878400)`. Note that the `lakes.shp` CRS uses square feet, and we therefore have to multiply by 27,878,400 to convert from square feet to square miles. The dialog will look like the following screenshot.
- We can also work with string functions, for example, to find lakes with long names (such as `length("NAMES") > 12`) or lakes with names that contain `s` or `S` (such as `lower("NAMES") LIKE '%s%'`); the string functions first convert the names to lowercase and then looks for any appearance of `s`.

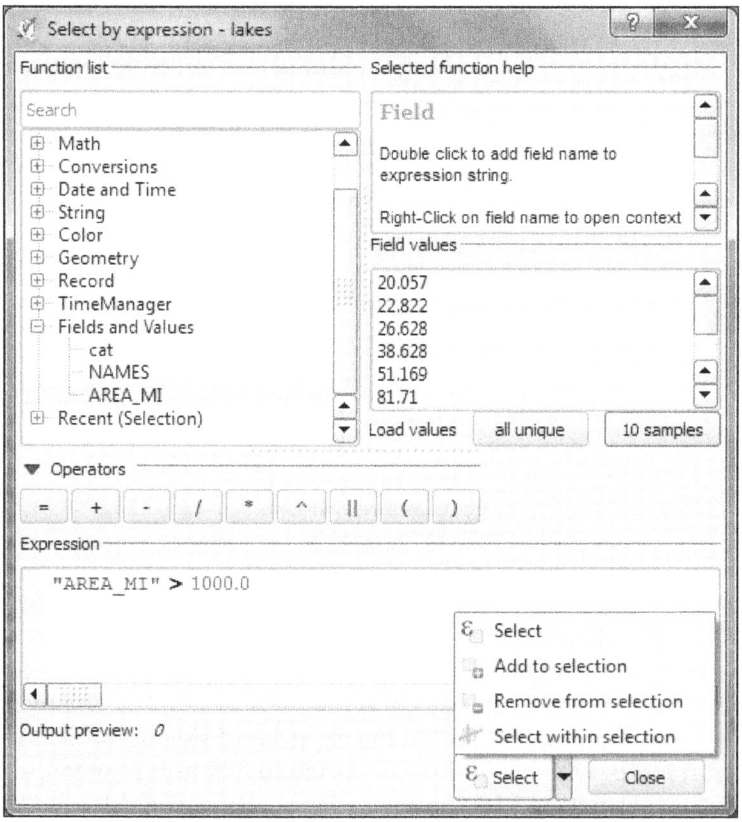

The third type of tool is called **Spatial Query** and allows us to select features in one layer based on their location relative to the features in a second layer. These tools can be accessed by going to **Vector** | **Research Tools** | **Select by location** and **Vector** | **Spatial Query** | **Spatial Query**. Enable it in **Plugin Manager** if you cannot find it in the **Vector** menu. In general, we want to use the Spatial Query plugin as it supports a variety of spatial operations such as **crosses**, **equals**, **intersects**, **is disjoint**, **overlaps**, **touches**, and **contains**, depending on the layer geometry type.

Let's test the Spatial Query plugin using `railroads.shp` and `pipelines.shp` from the sample data. For example, we might want to find all the railroad features that cross a pipeline; we therefore select the **railroads** layer, the **Crosses** operation, and the **pipelines** layer. After clicking on **Apply**, the plugin presents us with the query results. There is a list of IDs of the result features on the right-hand side of the window, as you can see in the following screenshot. Below this list, we can check the **Zoom to item** checkbox and QGIS will zoom to the feature that belongs to the selected ID. Additionally, the plugin offers buttons to directly save all the resulting features to a new layer.

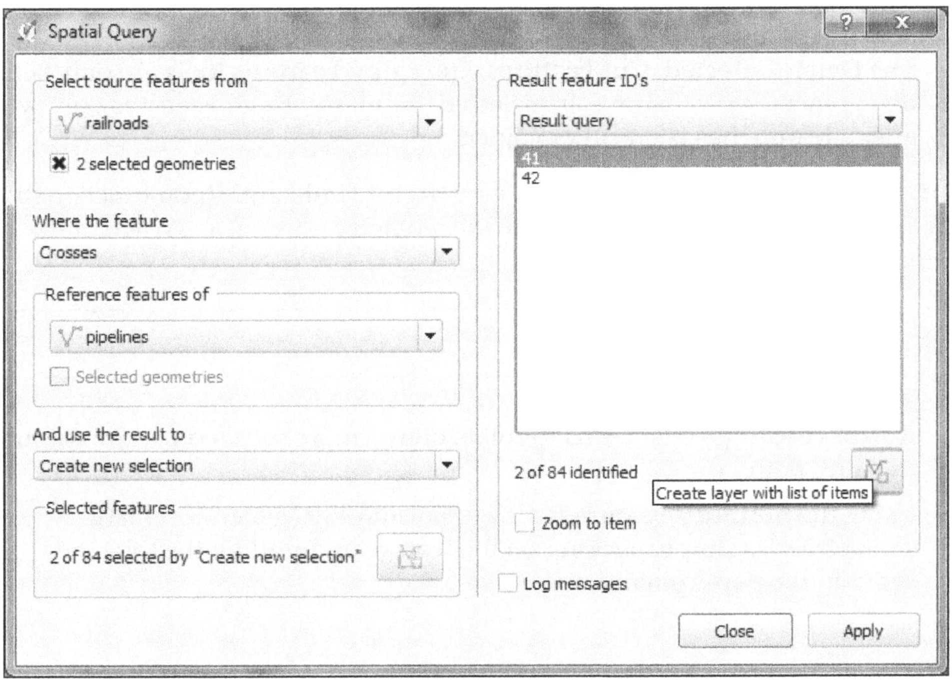

Editing vector geometries

Now that we know how to create and select features, we can have a closer look at the other tools in the **Digitizing** and **Advanced Digitizing** toolbars. The basic **Digitizing** toolbar—as shown in the following screenshot—contains tools to create and move features and nodes, as well as to delete, copy, cut, and paste features as follows:

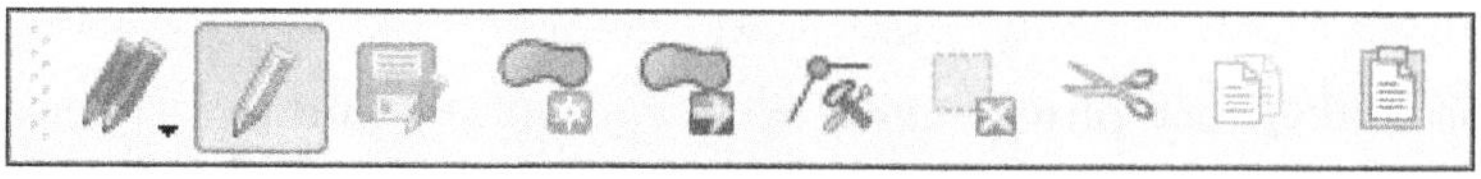

- With the **Move Feature(s)** tool, it is easy to move one or more features at once by dragging them to the new location.
- Similarly, the **Node Tool** feature allows us to move one or more nodes of the same feature. The first click activates the feature, while the second click selects the node. Hold the mouse key down to drag the node to its new location. Instead of moving only one node, we can also move an edge by clicking-and-dragging the line. Finally, we can select and move multiple nodes by holding down the *Ctrl* key.
- The **Delete Selected**, **Cut Features**, and **Copy Features** tools are only active if one or more layer features are selected. Similarly, **Paste Features** only works after a feature has been cut or copied.

The **Advanced Digitizing** toolbar offers very useful **Undo** and **Redo** functionalities as well as additional tools for more involved geometry editing, as shown in the following screenshot:

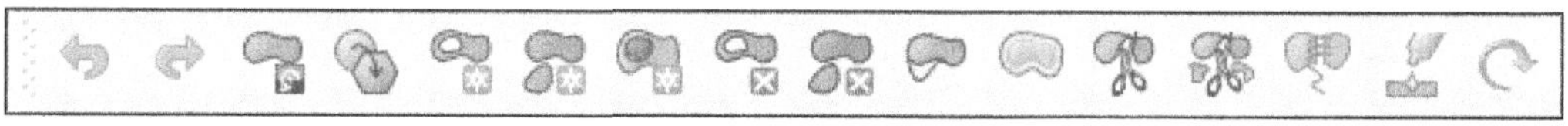

- **Rotate Feature(s)** enables us to rotate one or more selected features around a central point.
- Using the **Simplify Feature** tool, we can simplify/generalize feature geometries by simply clicking on the feature and pulling the tolerance slider in the pop-up window.

- The following tools can be used to modify polygons. They allow us to add rings, also known as *holes*, into the existing polygons or add parts to them. The **Fill Ring** tool is similar to **Add Ring**, but instead of just creating a hole, it also creates a new feature that fills the hole. Of course, there are tools to delete rings and parts as well.
- The **Reshape Features** tool can be used to alter the geometry of a feature by either cutting out or adding pieces. You can control the behavior by starting to draw the new form inside the original feature to add a piece or start outside to cut out a piece, as shown in the following example diagram:

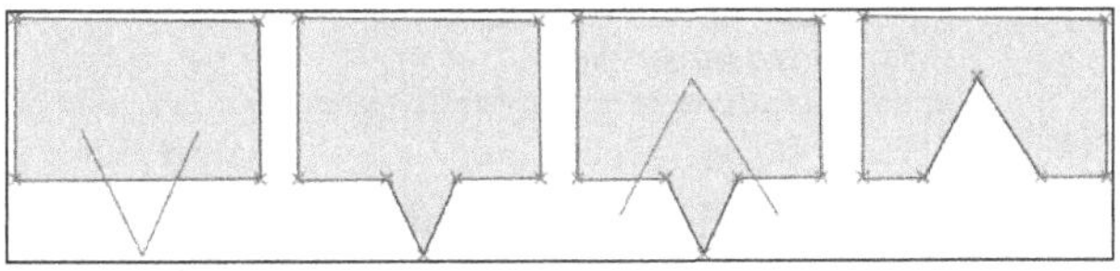

- The **Offset Curve** tool is only available for lines and allows us to displace a line geometry by a given offset.
- The **Split Features** tool allows us to split one or more features into multiple features along a cut line. Similarly, **Split Parts** allows us to split a feature into multiple parts, which still belong to the same multipolygon or multipolyline.
- The **Merge Selected Features** tool enables us to merge multiple features while keeping control over which feature's attributes will be available in the output feature.
- Similarly, **Merge Attributes of Selected Features** lets us combine the attributes of multiple features, but without merging them into one feature. Instead, all the original features remain as they were, but the attribute values are updated.
- Finally, **Rotate Point Symbols** is only available for point layers with the **Rotation field** feature enabled (we will cover this feature in *Chapter 5, Creating Great Maps*).

Using the measuring tools

Another core functionality of any GIS is the measurement tools. In QGIS, we find the tools to measure lines, areas, and angles in the **Attribute** toolbar, as shown in the following screenshot:

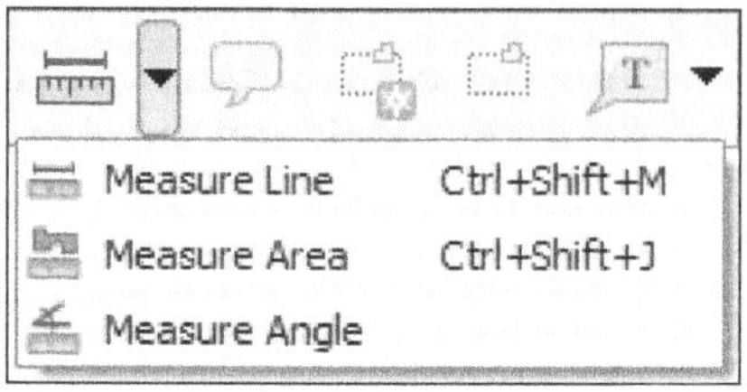

The measurements are updated continuously while we draw measurement lines, areas, or angles. When we draw a line with multiple segments, the tool will show the length of each segment as well as the total length of all the segments put together. To stop measuring, we can just right-click. If we want to change the measurement units from meters to feet or from degrees to radians, we can do this by going to **Settings** | **Options** | **Map Tools**.

Editing attributes

There are three main use cases for attribute editing:

- First, we might want to edit the attributes of one specific feature, for example, to fix a wrong name
- Second, we might want to edit the attributes of a group of features
- Third, we might want to change the attributes of all the features within a layer.

Editing attributes in the attribute table

All three use cases are covered by the functionality available through the attribute table. We can access it by going to **Layer** | **Open Attribute Table**, the **Open Attribute Table** button present in the **Attributes** toolbar, or in the layer name context menu.

To change the attribute values, we always have to enable editing first. Then, we can double-click on any cell in the attribute table to activate the input mode, as shown in the upper dialog of the following screenshot:

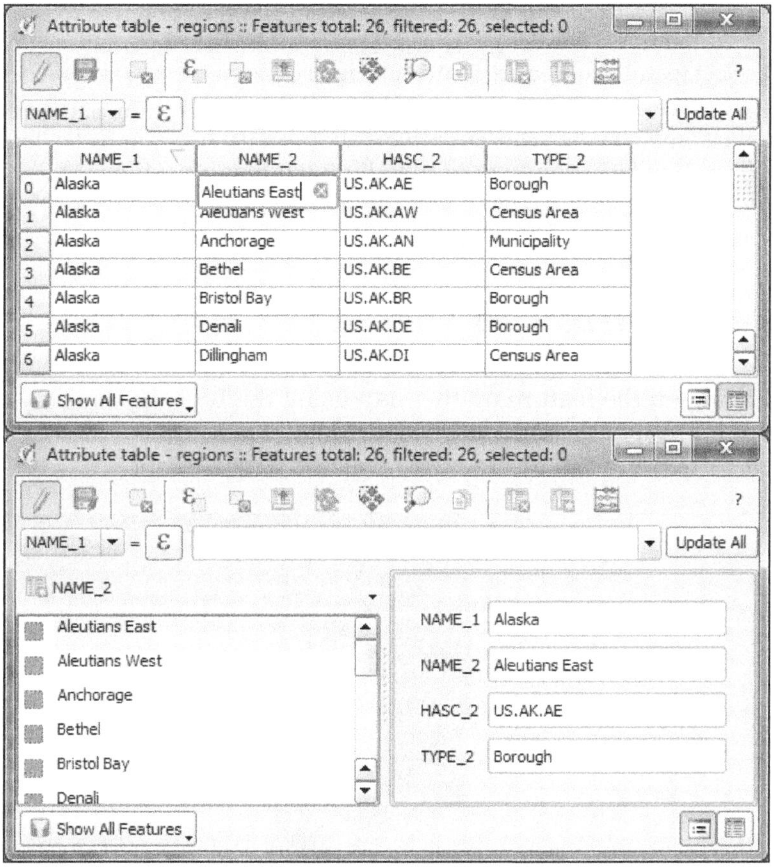

Pressing the *Enter* key confirms the change, but to save the new value permanently, we have to also click on the **Save Edit(s)** button or press *Ctrl* + *S*. Besides the classic attribute table view, QGIS also supports a form view, which you can see in the lower dialog of the previous screenshot. You can switch between these two views using the buttons in the bottom-right corner of the attribute table dialog box.

In the attribute table, we also find tools to handle selections (from left to right, starting at the third button): **Delete selected features**, **Select features using an expression**, **Unselect all**, **Move selection to top**, **Invert selection**, **Pan map to the selected rows**, **Zoom map to the selected rows**, and **Copy selected rows to clipboard**. Another way to select features in the attribute table is to click on the row number.

The next two buttons allow us to add and remove columns. When we click on the **Delete column** button, we get a list of columns to choose from. Similarly, the **New column** button brings up a dialog to specify the name and data type of the new column.

Editing attributes in the feature form

Another option to edit the attributes of one feature is to open the attribute form directly by clicking on the feature on the map using the **Identify tool**. By default, the **Identify tool** displays the attribute values in the read mode, but we can enable the **Auto open form** option in the **Identify Results** panel, as shown here:

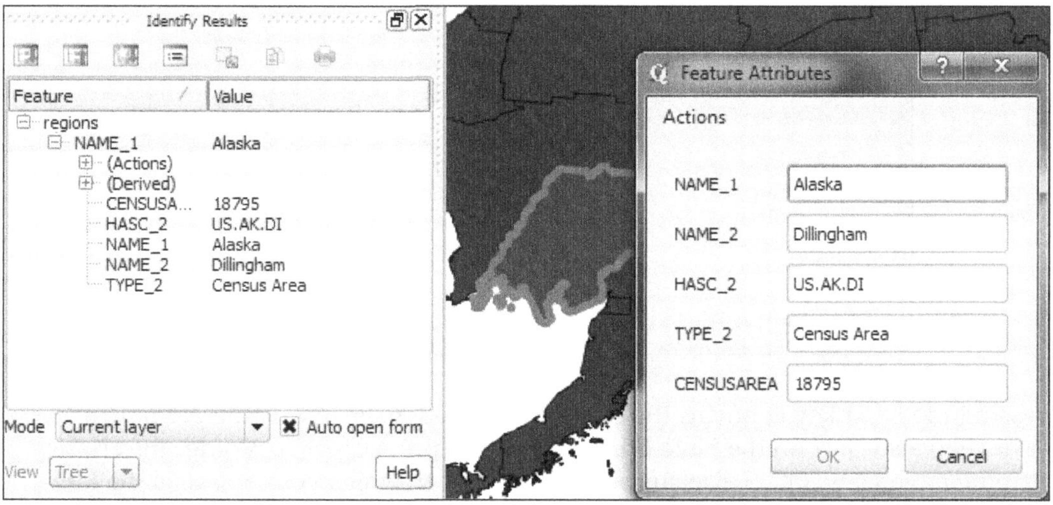

What you can see in the previous screenshot is the default feature-attributes form that QGIS creates automatically, but we are not limited to this basic form. By going to **Layer Properties | Fields section**, we can configure the look and feel of the form in more detail. The **Attribute editor layout** options are (in an increasing level of complexity) as follows:

- **Autogenerate**: This is the most basic option. You can assign a specific **Edit widget** and **Alias** for each field; this will replace the default input field and label in the form. For this example, we use the following edit widget types:
    - **Text Edit** supports inserting one or more lines of text.
    - **Unique Values** creates a drop-down list that allows the user to select one of the values already used in the attribute table. If the **Editable** option is activated, the drop-down list is replaced by a text edit widget with autocompletion support.
    - **Range** creates an edit widget for numeric values from a specific range.

> For the complete list of available edit widget types, refer to the user manual at `http://docs.qgis.org/2.2/en/docs/user_manual/working_with_vector/vector_properties.html#fields-menu`.

- **Drag and drop designer**: This allows further control of the form layout. As you can see in the following screenshot, the designer enables us to create tabs within the form and also makes it possible to change the order of the form fields. The workflow is as follows:
    1. Click on the plus button to add one or more tabs (for example, a `Region` tab, as shown in the following screenshot).
    2. On the left-hand side of the dialog, select the field you want to add to the form.
    3. On the right-hand side, select the tab to which you want to add the field.
    4. Press the button with the icon of an arrow pointing to the right to add the selected field to the selected tab.

5. You can reorder the fields in the form using the up and down arrow buttons or—as the name suggests—by dragging-and-dropping the fields up or down.

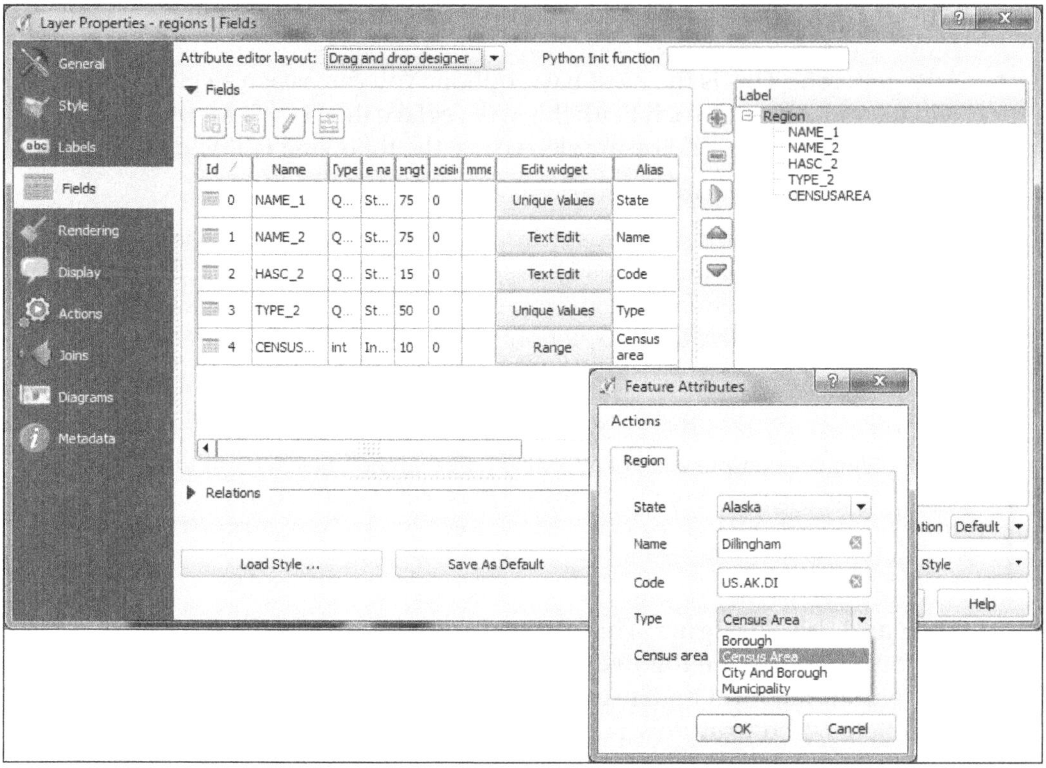

- **Provide ui-file**: This is the most advanced option. It enables you to use a Qt user interface designed using, for example, the Qt Designer software. This allows a great deal of freedom in designing the form layout and behavior.

> Creating `.ui` files is out of the scope of this book, but you can find more information at `http://docs.qgis.org/2.2/en/docs/training_manual/create_vector_data/forms.html#hard-fa-creating-a-new-form`.

Calculating new attribute values

If we want to change the attributes of multiple or all features in a layer, editing them manually usually isn't an option. This is what **Field calculator** is good for. We can access it using the **Open field calculator** button in the attribute table or by pressing *Ctrl + I*. In **Field calculator**, we can choose to only update selected features or update all the features in the layer. Besides updating an existing field, we can also create a new field. The function list is the same one that we already explored when we selected features by expression. We can use any of these functions to populate a new field or update an existing one. Here are some example expressions that are used often:

- We can create an `id` column using the `$rownum` function, which populates a column with the row numbers, as shown in the following screenshot:

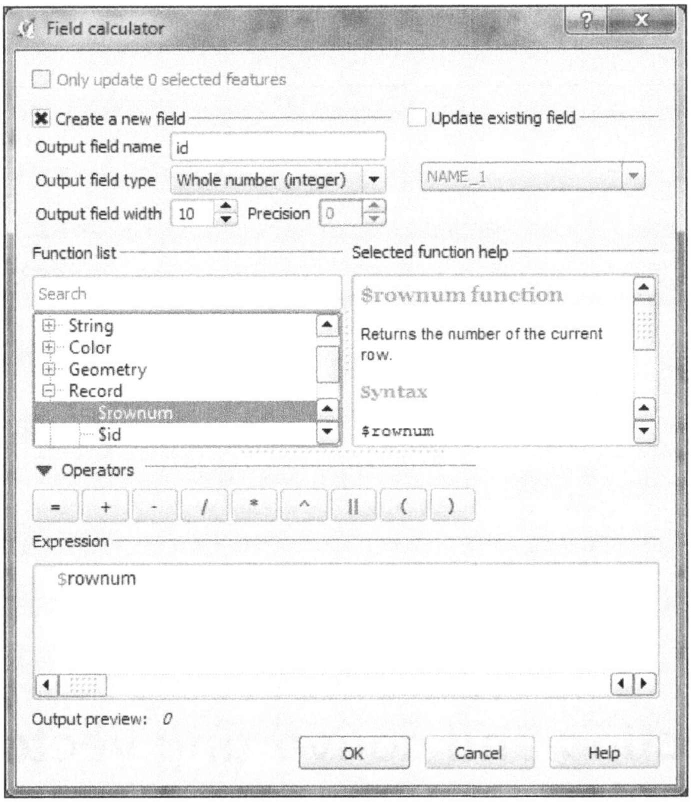

- Another common use case is to calculate the line length or polygon area using the `$length` and `$area` geometry functions, respectively
- Similarly, we can get point coordinates using `$x` and `$y`
- If we want to get the start or endpoint of a line, we can use `xat(0)` and `yat(0)` respectively or `xat(-1)` and `yat(-1)` respectively

An alternative to the **Field calculator**—especially if you already know the formula you want to use—is the field calculator bar, which you can find directly in the **Attribute table** dialog right below the toolbar. In the following screenshot, you can see an example that calculates the area of all the census areas: It uses a `CASE WHEN - THEN - END` expression to check if the value of `TYPE_2` is `Census Area`:

```
CASE WHEN TYPE_2 = 'Census Area' THEN $area / 27878400 END
```

Enter the formula and click on the **Update All** button to execute it:

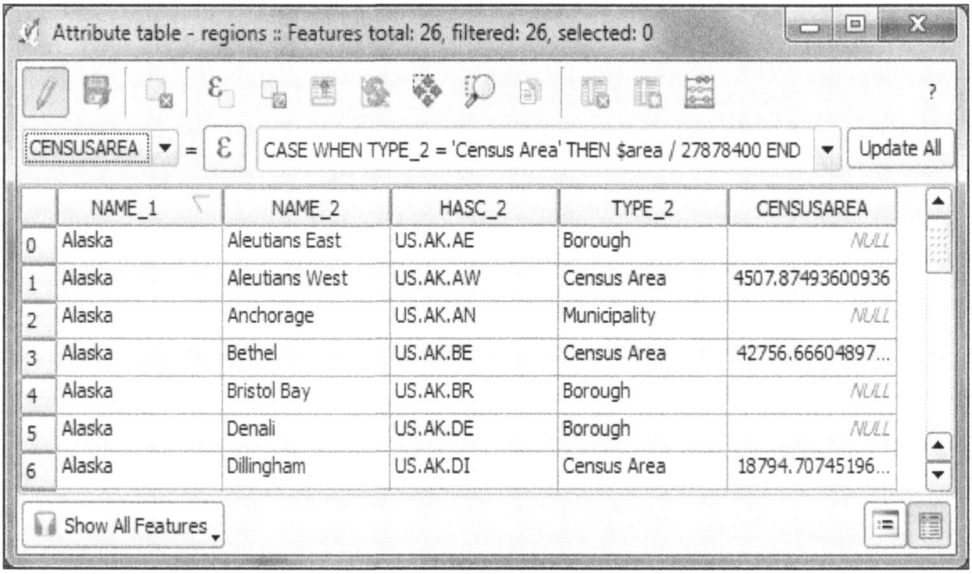

Reprojecting and converting vector and raster data

In *Chapter 2, Viewing Spatial Data*, we talked about CRS and the fact that QGIS offers on-the-fly reprojection to display spatial datasets, which are stored in a different CRS, in the same map. Still, in some cases, we might want to permanently reproject a dataset, for example, to geoprocess it later on.

In QGIS, reprojecting a vector or raster layer is done by simply saving it with a new CRS. We can save a layer by going to **Layer** | **Save as...** or **Save as...** in the layer name context menu. Pick a target file format and filename, and then click on the **Change** button beside the CRS field to pick a new CRS.

Besides changing the CRS, the main use case of the Save vector/raster layer dialog, as depicted in the following screenshot, is to convert between different file formats. For example, we can load a Shapefile and export it as GeoJSON, Mapinfo MIF, CSV, and so on, or the other way around.

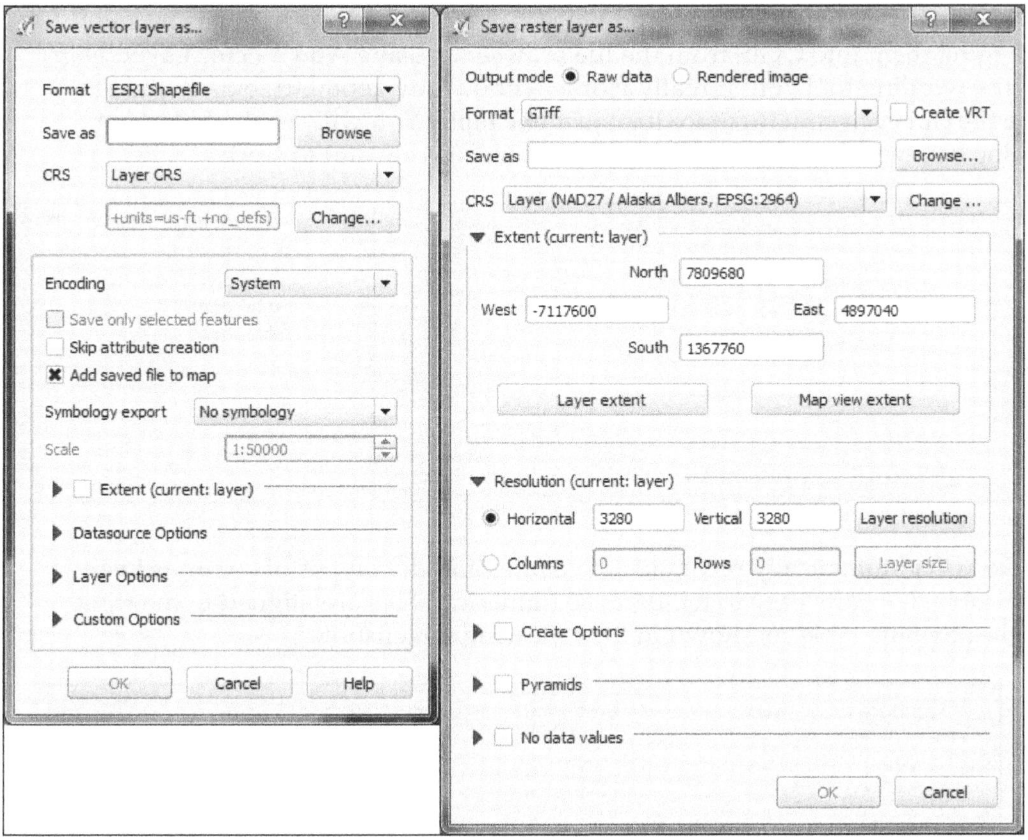

The **Save raster layer** dialog is also a convenient way to clip/crop rasters by a bounding box, as we can specify which extent we want to save.

Furthermore, the **Save vector layer** dialog features a **Save only selected features** option, which will enable us to save only the selected features instead of all the features of the layer (this option is only available if there are actually some selected features in the layer).

> Enabling **Add saved file to map** (currently only available in the vector dialog) is very convenient because it saves us the effort of going and loading the new file manually after it has been saved.

Joining tabular data

In many real-life situations, we get additional non-spatial data in the form of spreadsheets or text files. The good news is that we can load XLS files by simply dragging them into QGIS from the file browser or using **Add Vector Layer**. Don't let the wording fool you! It really works without any geometry data in the file. The file can even contain more than just one table. You will see the following dialog box, which lets you choose which table(s) you want to load:

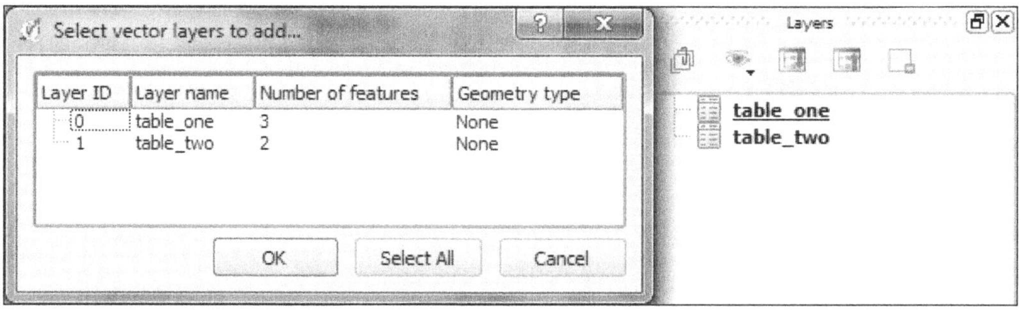

QGIS will automatically recognize the names and data types of columns in an XLS table. It's quite easy to tell because numeric values are aligned to the right in the attribute table, as shown in the following screenshot:

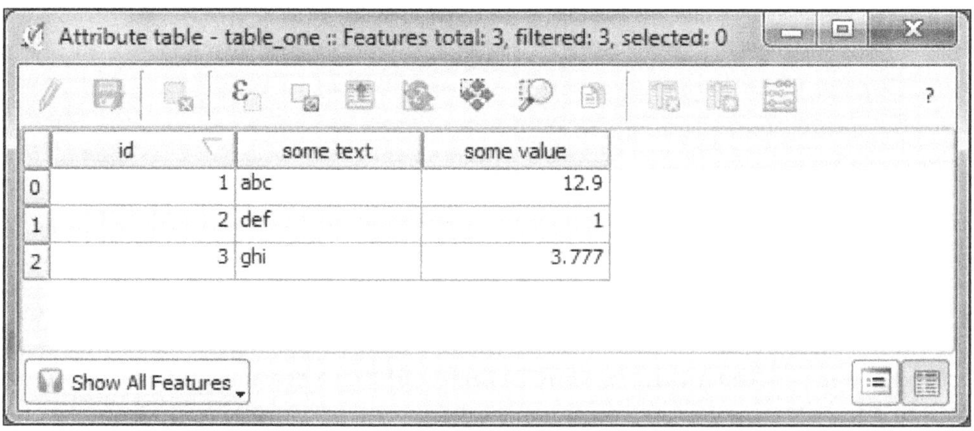

We can also load tabular data from delimited text files, like we saw in *Chapter 2, Viewing Spatial Data*, when we loaded a point layer from a delimited text file. To load a delimited text file that only contains tabular data but no geometry information, we just need to enable the **No geometry** (attribute table only) option.

After loading the tabular data from either the spreadsheet or text file, we can continue to join this non-spatial data to a vector layer. To do this, we can navigate to the vector **Layer Properties | Joins**. Here, we can add a new join by pressing the green plus button. All we have to do is select the tabular **Join layer** and **Join field** fields (of the tabular layer), which will contain values that match those in the **Target field** field (of the vector layer). Additionally, we can—if we want to—choose which fields are joined by enabling the **Choose which fields are joined** option and selecting the desired subset of fields. For example, the settings shown in the following screenshot will only add the `some value` field:

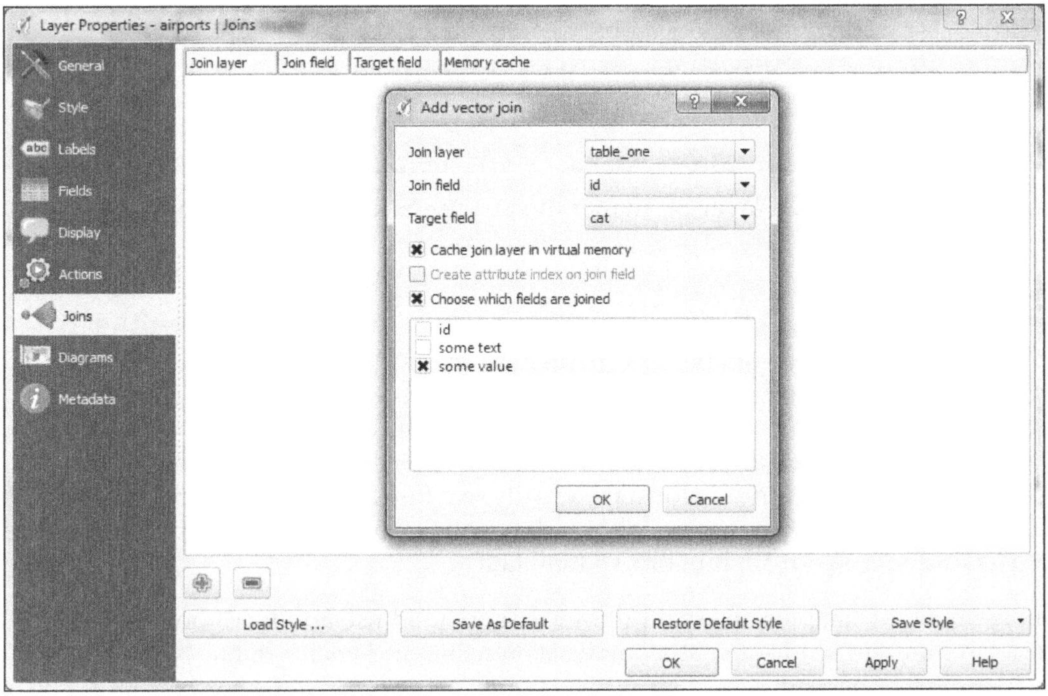

Once the join is added, we can see the extended attribute table and use the new appended attributes (as shown in the following screenshot) for styling and labeling. The way joins work in QGIS is that the join layer's attributes are appended to the original layer's attribute table. The number of features in the original layer is not changed. Whenever there is a match between the join and the target field, the attribute value will be filled; otherwise, you'll see NULL entries.

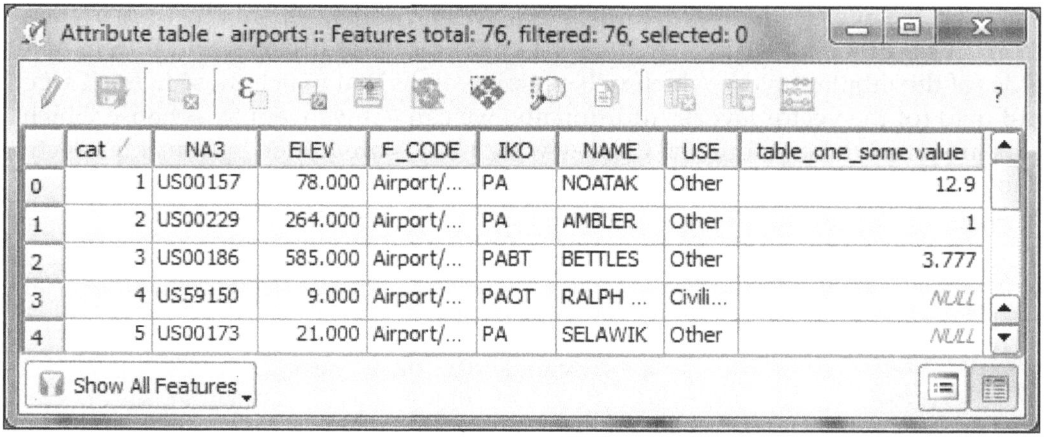

You can save the joined layer permanently; just use **Save as...** to create the new file.

Summary

In this chapter, you learned how to create new layers from scratch. We used the tools to create and edit feature geometries in different ways. Then, we went into editing feature attributes of single features, feature selections, and whole layers. Next, we reprojected both the vector and raster layers and also learned how to convert between different file formats. Finally, we finished this chapter with layer creation and editing by covering tabular data and learning how it can be loaded into QGIS and how to join it to our spatial data.

In the following chapter, we will put our data to good use and learn how to perform different kinds of spatial analysis on raster and vector data.

4
Spatial Analysis

In this chapter, we will start with raster processing and analysis tasks such as clipping and terrain analysis. We will cover the essentials of converting between the raster and vector formats and then continue with common vector geoprocessing tasks such as generating heatmaps and calculating area shares within a region. We will finish the chapter with an introduction to automating geoprocessing workflows using the QGIS Processing modeler.

Clipping rasters

A common task in raster processing is clipping a raster with a polygon. This task is well covered by the Clipper tool, which can be accessed by going to **Raster | Extraction | Clipper**. This tool supports clipping to a specified extent or clipping using a polygon mask layer as follows:

- The extent can be set manually or by selecting it in the map. To do this, we can just click-and-drag the mouse to open a rectangle in the map area of the main QGIS window.
- A mask layer can be any polygon layer that is currently loaded in the project or any other polygon layer that can be specified using **Select...** right next to the **Mask layer** drop-down list.

> If we only want to clip a raster to a certain extent (the current map view extent or any other), we can also use the raster **Save as ...** option, as shown in *Chapter 3, Data Creation and Editing*.

For a quick exercise, we will clip the hillshade raster (`SR_50M_alaska_nad.tif`) using the Alaska shapefile (both from our sample data) as a mask layer. At the bottom of the window, as shown in the following screenshot, we can see the concrete `gdalwarp` command that QGIS uses to clip the raster. This is very useful if you want to learn how to use GDAL.

> In *Chapter 2, Viewing Spatial Data*, we already discussed that GDAL is one of the libraries QGIS uses to read and process raster data. You can find the documentation of `gdalwarp` and all the other GDAL utility programs at `http://www.gdal.org/gdal_utilities.html`.

The default **No data value** option is the no data value used in the input data set or **0** if nothing is specified, but we can override this value if necessary. Another good option is to create an output alpha band, which will set all the areas outside the mask to transparent. This will add an additional band to the output raster; this band controls the transparency of the rendered raster cells.

A common error source is to forget to add the file format extension to the output file (in our example, `.tif` for GeoTiff). Similarly, you would get errors if you try to overwrite an existing file. In this case, the best way to fix this is to either choose a different filename or delete the existing file first.

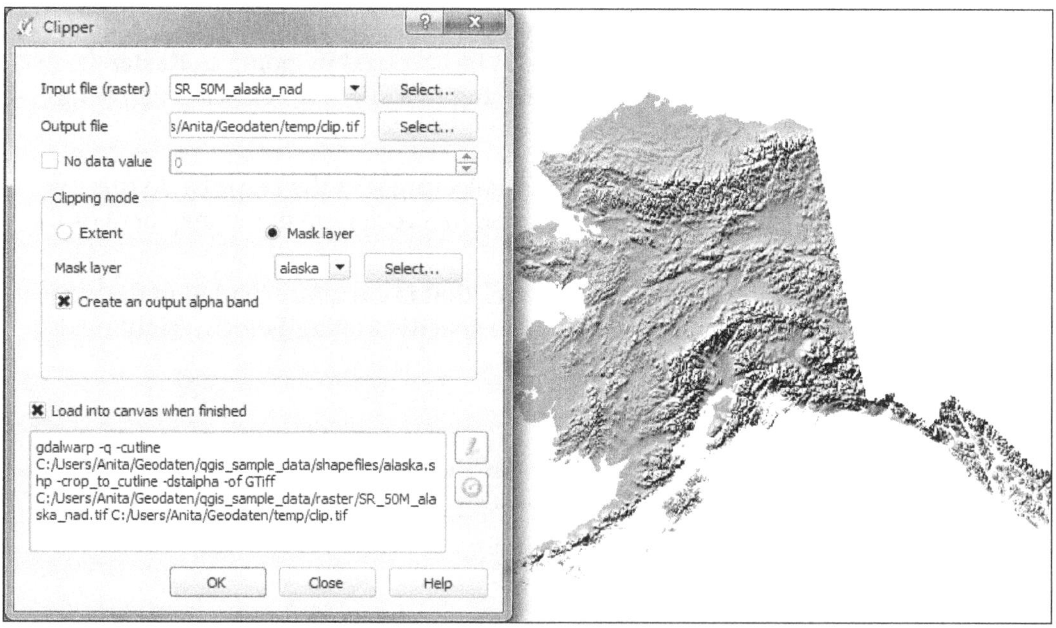

The resulting layer will be loaded automatically, since we enabled the **Load into canvas when finished** option. QGIS should also automatically recognize the alpha layer we created, and the raster areas that fall outside the Alaska land mass should be transparent, as shown on the right-hand side of the previous screenshot. If, for some reason, QGIS fails to automatically recognize the alpha layer, we can enable it manually using the **Transparency band** option in the **Transparency** section of raster layer properties, as shown in the following screenshot. This dialog box is also the right place to specify any no data value that we might want to be used.

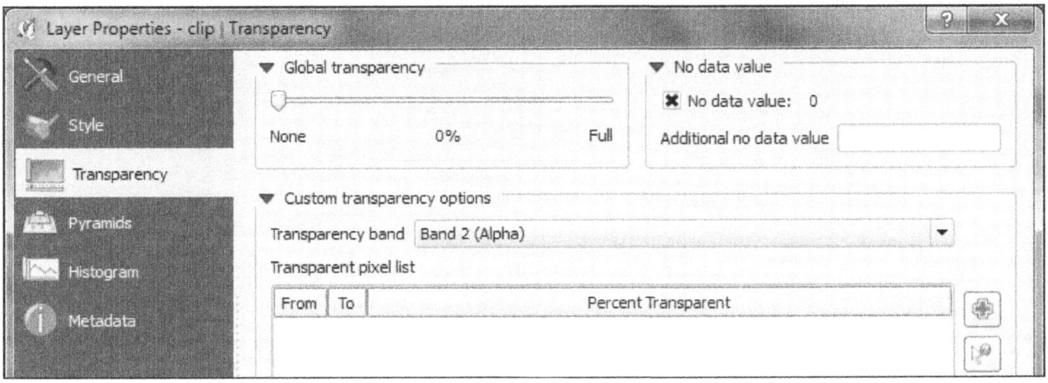

Analyzing elevation / terrain data

To use terrain-analysis tools, we need an elevation raster. If you don't have any at hand, you can simply download a dataset from the NASA **Shuttle Radar Topography Mission (SRTM)** at `http://dwtkns.com/srtm/` or from any of the other SRTM download services.

> If you want to exactly replicate the results in the following exercise, get the dataset called `srtm_05_01.zip`, which covers a small part of Alaska.

Raster terrain analysis can be used to calculate the slope, aspect, hillshade, ruggedness index, and relief from elevation rasters, as shown in the following screenshot. These tools can be accessed by going to **Raster** | **Terrain analysis**, which comes with QGIS by default, but we have to enable it in the plugin manager.

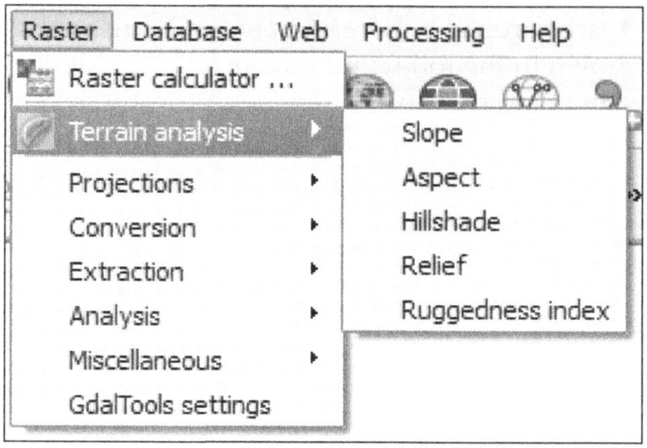

The terrain analysis plugin includes the following tools:

- **Slope**: This tool calculates the slope angle for each cell in degrees (based on the first-order derivative estimation)
- **Aspect**: This tool calculates the exposition (in degrees, counter-clockwise, starting with **0** for north)
- **Hillshade**: This tool creates a basic hillshade raster with lighted areas and shadows
- **Relief**: This tool creates a shaded relief map with varying colors for different elevation ranges
- **Ruggedness Index**: This tool calculates the ruggedness index for each cell by summarizing the elevation changes within a 3 x 3 cell grid

An important element in all terrain analysis tools is the **Z factor**. The Z factor is used if the *x*/*y* units are different from the z (elevation) unit. For example, if we tried to create a relief from elevation data where x/y are in degrees and *z* is in meters, the resulting relief would look grossly exaggerated. The values for the Z factor are as follows:

- If x/y and z are either all in meters or all in feet, use the default z factor, `1.0`
- If x/y are in degrees and z is in feet, use the z factor, `370,400`
- If x/y are in degrees and z is in meters, use the z factor, `111,120`

Since the SRTM rasters are provided in WGS84 EPSG:4326, we need to use a **Z factor** value of `111,120` in our exercise. Let's create a relief! The tool can calculate relief color ranges automatically; we just need to click on **Create automatically**, as shown in the following screenshot. Of course, we can still edit the elevation ranges' upper and lower bounds as well as the colors.

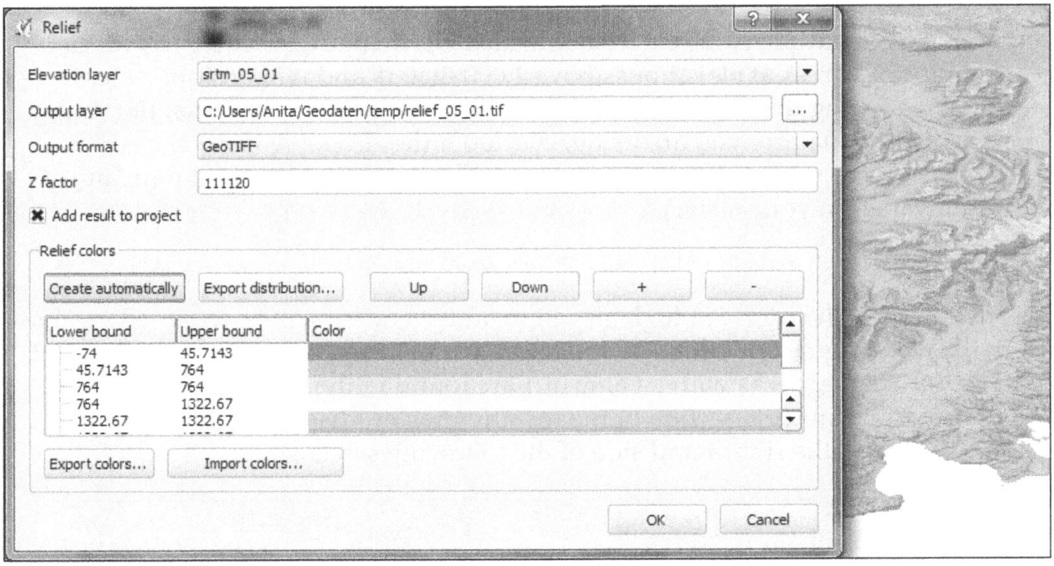

While relief maps are three-banded rasters, which are primarily used for visualization purposes, slope rasters are a common intermediate step in spatial analysis workflows. We will now create a slope raster, which we can use in our example workflow, in the following sections. The resulting slope raster will be loaded in grayscale automatically, as shown in the following screenshot:

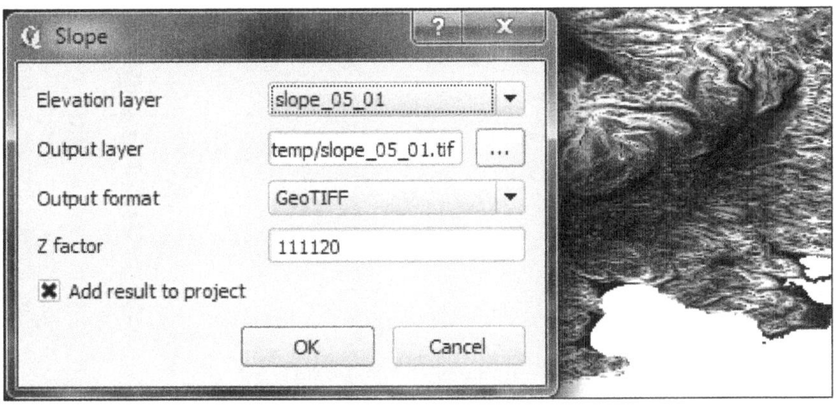

Raster calculator

By going to **Raster** | **Raster Calculator**, we can create a new raster layer based on the values in one or more rasters that are loaded in the current QGIS project. All the available raster bands are presented in a list in the top-left corner of the dialog in the `raster_name@band_number` form.

Continuing from our previous exercise in which we created a slope raster, we can, for example, find areas at elevations above 1,000 meters and with a slope of less than 5 degrees using the following expression (you might have to adjust the values depending on the dataset you are using; check out the *Accessing raster and vector layer statistics* section later in this chapter to learn how to find the minimum and maximum values in your raster):

```
"srtm_05_01@1" > 1000 AND "slope_05_01@1" < 5
```

Cells that meet both criteria of high elevation and evenness will be assigned a value of 1 in the resulting raster, while cells that fail to meet even one criterion will be set to 0. The only bigger areas with a value of 1 are found in the southern part of the raster layer. You can see a section of the resulting raster (displayed in black over the relief layer) on the right-hand side of the following screenshot:

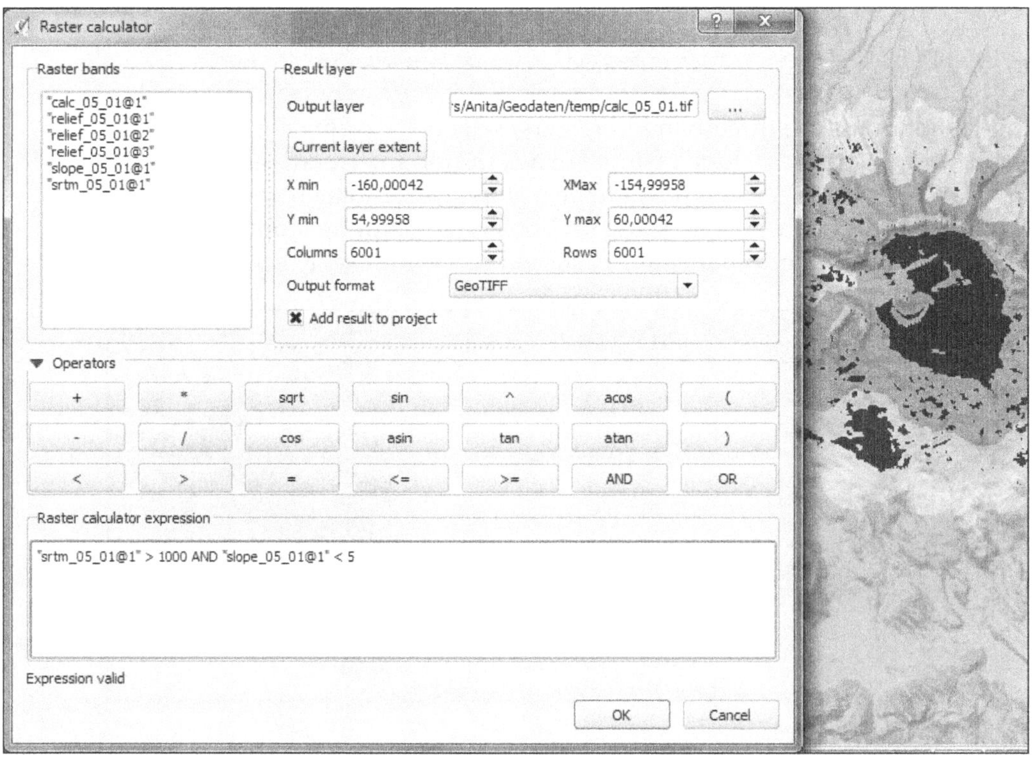

Another typical use case is reclassifying a raster. For example, we might want to reclassify the `landcover.img` raster in our sample data so that all the areas with a `landcover` class from `1` to `5` get the value of `100`, areas from `6` to `10` get the value of `101`, and areas over `11` get a new value of `102`. We will use the following code for this:

```
("landcover@1" > 0 AND "landcover@1" <= 6 ) * 100
+ ("landcover@1" >= 7 AND "landcover@1" <= 10 ) * 101
+ ("landcover@1" >= 11 ) * 102
```

The preceding raster-calculator expression has three parts that consist of a check and a multiplication. For each cell, only one of the three checks can be true, and true is represented as 1. Therefore, if a `landcover` cell has a value of `4`, the first check will be true, and the expression evaluates to `1*100 + 0*101 + 0*102 = 100`.

Converting between rasters and vectors

Tools to convert between the raster and vector formats can be accessed by going to **Raster | Conversion**; these tools are called **Rasterize (Vector to raster)** and **Polygonize (Raster to vector)**. Like the raster clipper tool we used earlier, this tool is also based on GDAL and displays the command at the bottom of the dialog.

Polygonize converts a raster into a polygon layer; depending on the size of the raster, the conversion can take some time. When the process is finished, QGIS will notify us with a pop up. For a quick test, we can, for example, convert the reclassified `landcover` raster to polygons. The resulting vector polygon layer contains multiple polygon features with a single attribute that we named `lc`, which depends on the original raster value, as shown in the following screenshot:

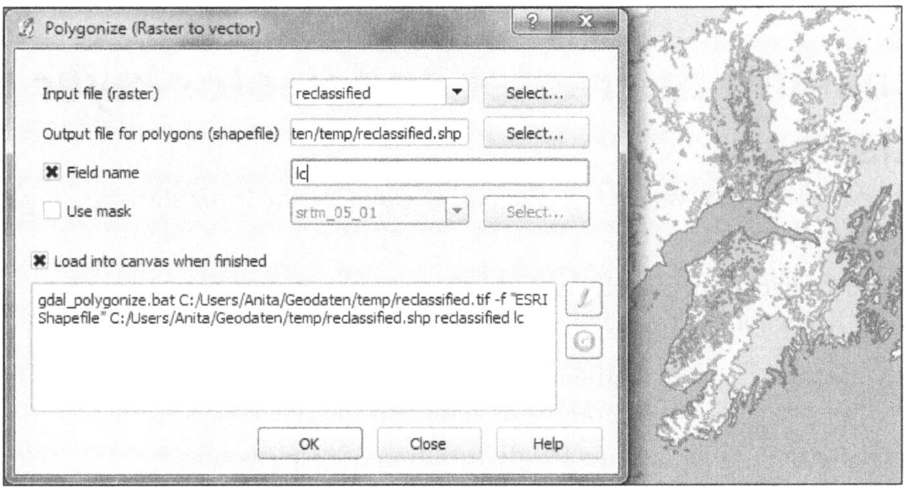

The **Rasterize** tool is very similar to the **Polygonize** tool. The only difference is that we get to specify the size of the resulting raster in pixels/cells. We can also specify the attribute field, which will provide input for the raster cell value. The **cat** attribute of our `alaska.shp` dataset is rather meaningless, but you get an idea of how the tool works, as shown in the following screenshot:

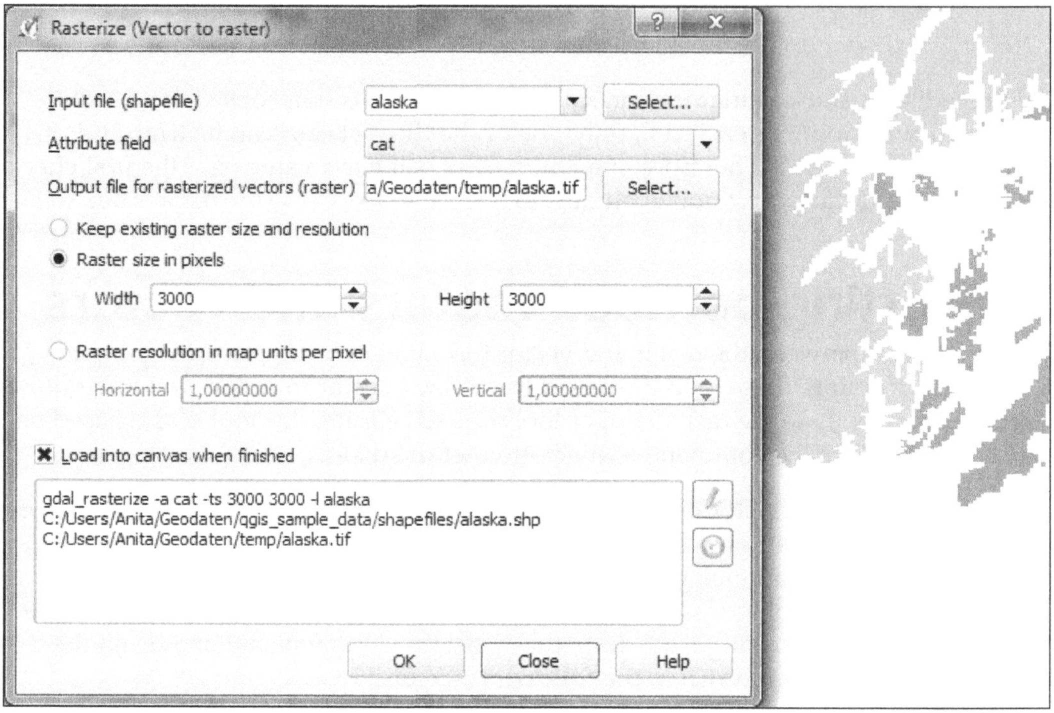

Accessing the raster and vector layer statistics

Whenever we get a new dataset, it is useful to examine the layer statistics to get a feeling for the data.

Raster layer statistics are readily available in the **Layer Properties** dialog box, specifically in the following tabs:

- **Metadata**: This shows the minimum and maximum cell values as well as the mean and the standard deviation of the cell values
- **Histogram**: This presents the distribution of raster values

For vector layers, we can get summary statistics using two tools that can be accessed by going to **Vector** | **Analysis Tools**:

- **Basics statistics**: This is very useful for numeric fields. It calculates parameters such as mean and median, min and max, the feature count *n* and the number of unique values, and so on for all the features of a layer or for the selected features only.
- **List unique values**: This is useful to get all the unique values of a certain field.

In both the tools, we can easily copy the results using *Ctrl* + *C* and paste them into a text file or spreadsheet. The following screenshots show examples that explore the contents of our airport sample dataset:

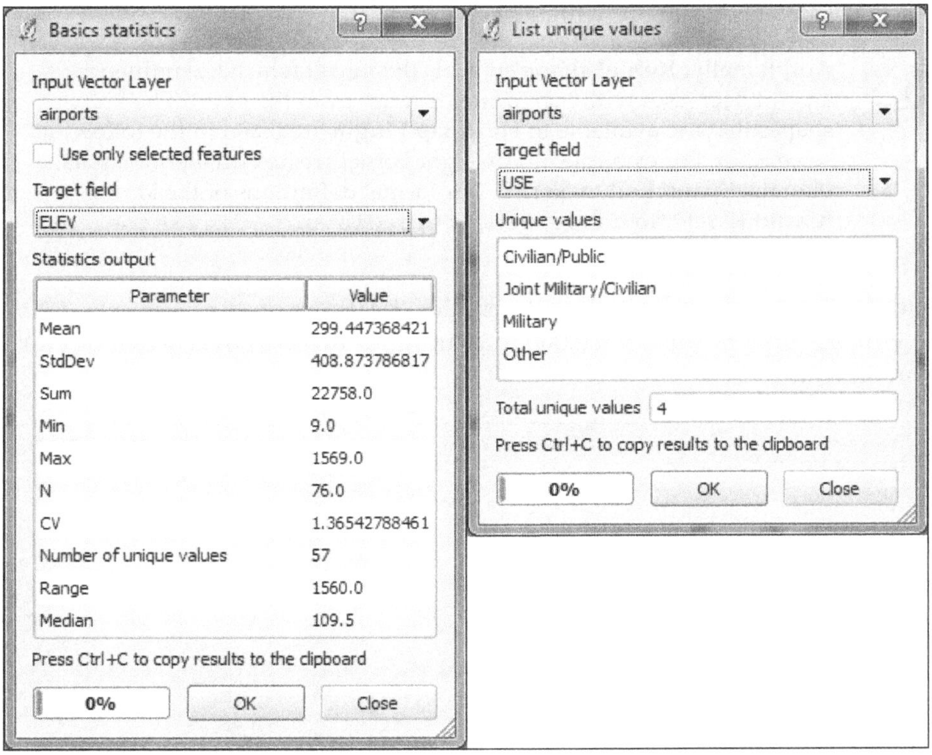

Creating a heatmap from points

Heatmaps are a great way to visualize the distribution of points. To create them, QGIS provides a simple-to-use **Heatmap Plugin** that we have to activate in **Plugin Manager**, and then we can access it by going to **Raster** | **Heatmap** | **Heatmap**. The plugin offers different Kernel shapes to choose from. The kernel is a moving window of a specific size and shape; this window moves over an area of points to calculate their local density. Additionally, the plugin allows us to control the output heatmap raster size in cells (the **Rows** and **Columns** settings) as well as the cell size.

> **Radius** determines the distance around each point at which the point will have an influence. Therefore, smaller radius values result in heatmaps that show finer smaller details, while larger values result in smoother heatmaps with fewer details.
>
> Additionally, **Kernel shape** controls the rate at which the influence of a point decreases with increasing distance from the point. The kernel shapes that are available in **Heatmap Plugin** are listed in the following screenshot. For example, a Triweight kernel creates smaller hotspots than the Epanechnikov kernel. For formal definitions of the kernel functions, refer to `http://en.wikipedia.org/wiki/Kernel_(statistics)`.

The following screenshot shows how to create a heatmap of our `airports.shp` sample with a kernel radius of 300,000 map units, which—in the case of our airport data—are in feet:

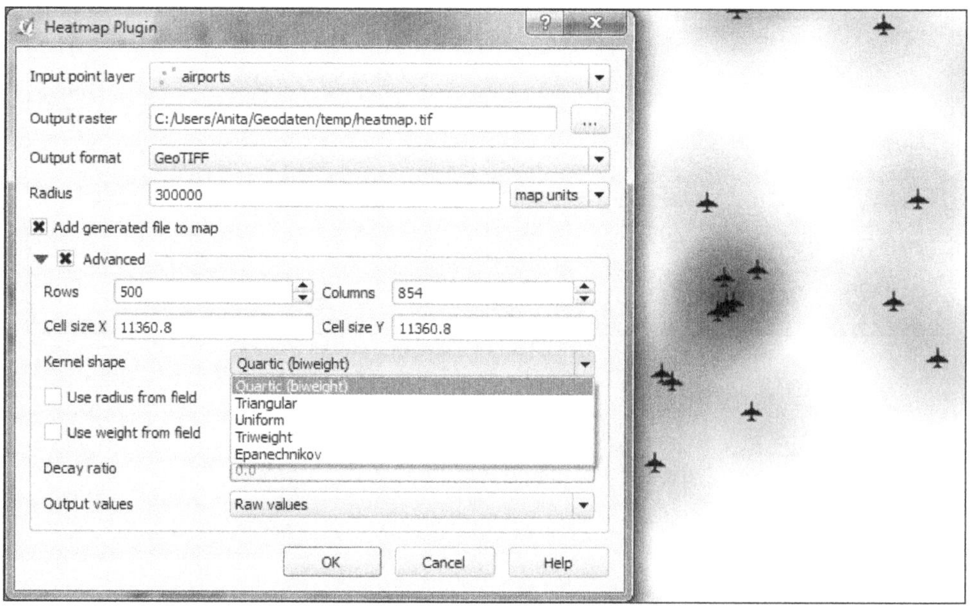

By default, the heatmap output will be rendered using the **Singleband greygray** render type (with low values in black and high values in white). To change the style to something similar to what you saw in the previous screenshot, you can perform the following steps:

1. Change the heatmap raster layer render type to **Singleband pseudocolor**.
2. In **Generate new color map section** on the right-hand side of the dialog box, select a color map you like, for example, the **PuRd** color map, as shown in the following screenshot.
3. You can enter the **Min** and **Max** values for the color map manually or have them computed by clicking on **Load** in the **Load min/max values** section.
4. Click on **Classify** to add the color map classes to the list on the left-hand side of the dialog box.
5. Optionally, change the color of the first entry (for the value `0`) to white (by double-clicking on the color in the list) to get a smooth transition from the white map background to our heatmap:

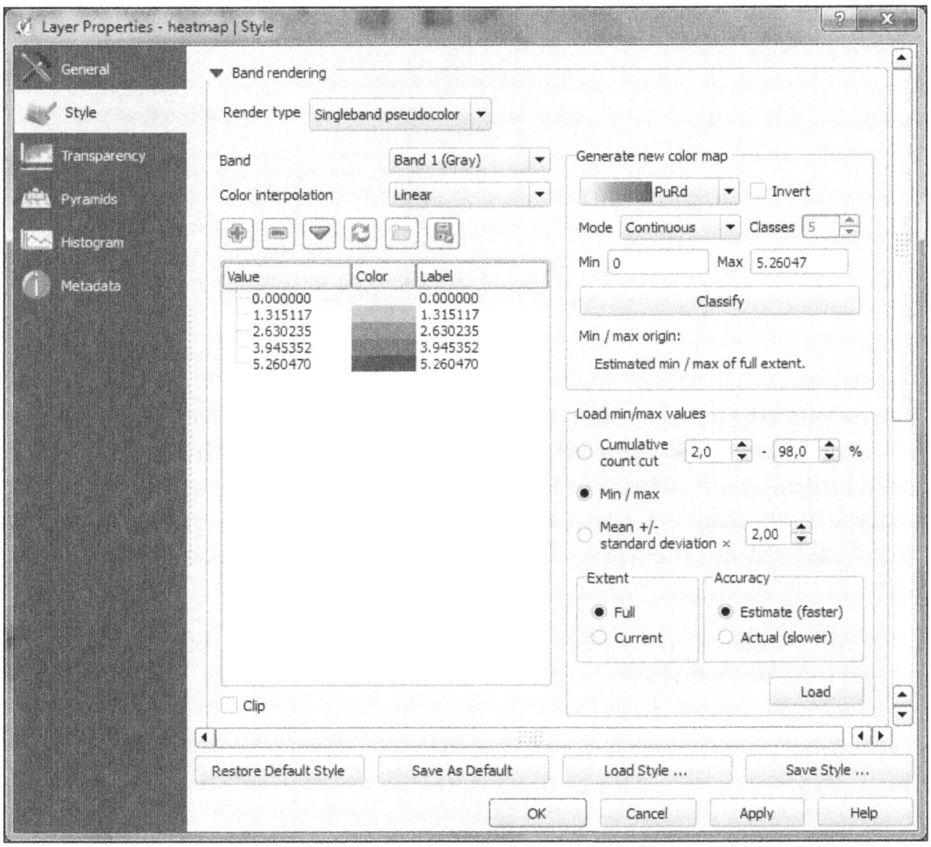

Vector geoprocessing using Processing

The most comprehensive set of spatial analysis tools is accessible via the Processing plugin, which we can also enable in the **Plugin Manager**. When the plugin is enabled, we will find a **Processing** menu where we can activate the **Toolbox**, as shown in the following screenshot. In the toolbox, it is easy to find spatial analysis tools by their names, thanks to the dynamic **Search** box at the top. This makes finding tools in the toolbox easier than in the vector or raster menu. Another advantage of getting accustomed to the Processing tools is that they can be automated in Python and in geoprocessing models.

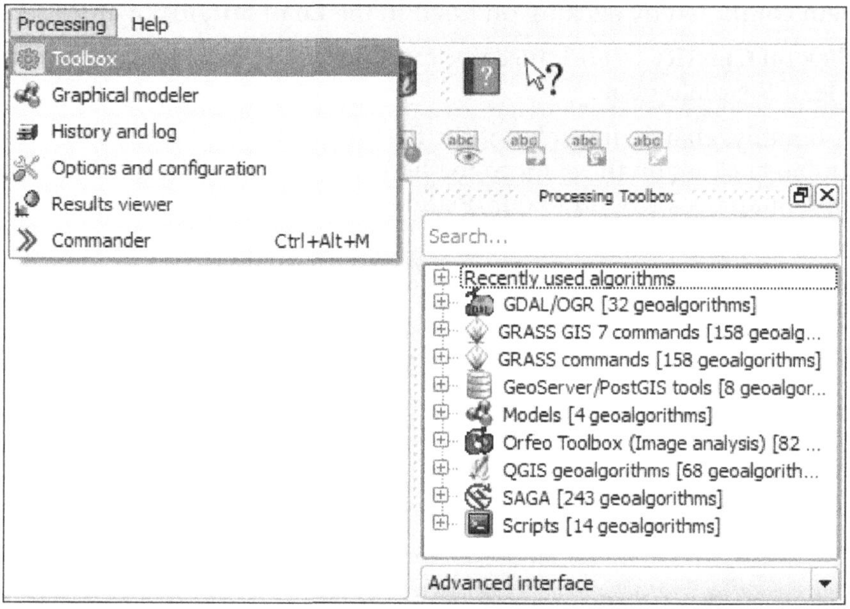

Note that the preceding screenshot shows the advanced interface of the toolbox. You can switch from the **Simplified interface** to the **Advanced interface** using the drop-down button at the bottom of the toolbox. It is recommended that you use the advanced version, as it exposes all the available algorithms and clearly displays how individual tools are related to the different components such as GDAL/OGR or GRASS.

In the upcoming sections, we will cover a selection of the available geoprocessing tools and see how we can use the modeler to automate our tasks.

Identifying features in the proximity of others

One common spatial analysis task is to identify features in the proximity of certain other features. One example is to find all the airports near rivers. Using `airports.shp` and `majrivers.shp` from our sample data, we can find airports within 5,000 feet of a river using a combination of the **Fixed distance buffer** and **Select by location** tools, as shown in the following screenshot:

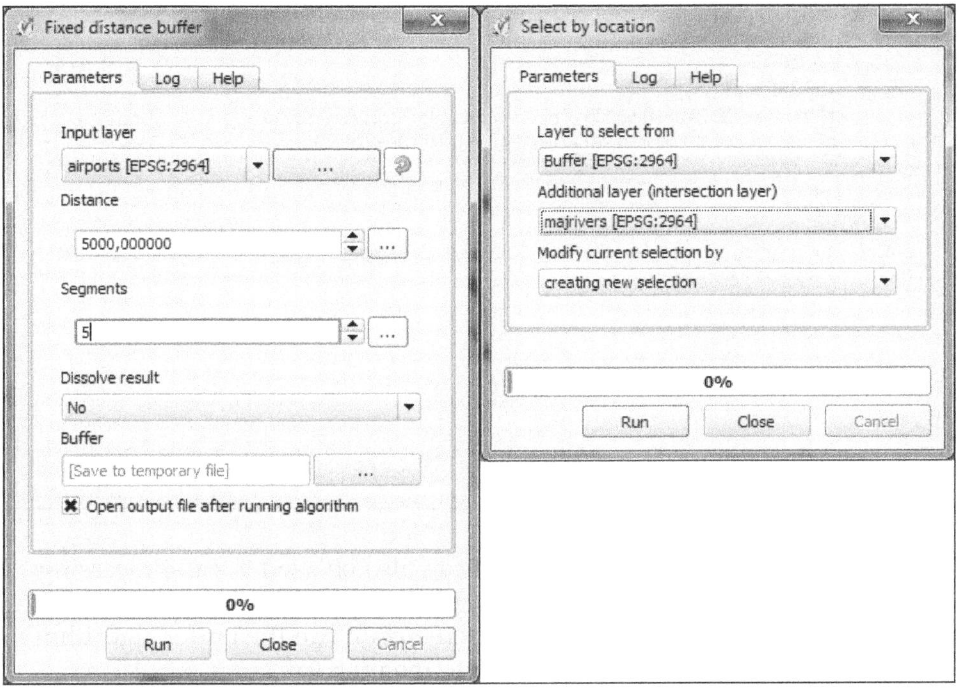

After buffering the airport point locations, the **Select by location** option selects all the airport buffers that intersect a river. As a result, 14 out of the 76 airports are selected. This information is displayed in the information area at the bottom of the QGIS main window, as shown in the following screenshot:

If you ever forget which settings you used or need to check whether you used the correct input layer, you can go to **Processing** | **History and log**. The **ALGORITHM** section lists all the algorithms we have been running as well as the used settings, as shown in the following screenshot. This is also the right place to look for error messages in the **ERROR** section.

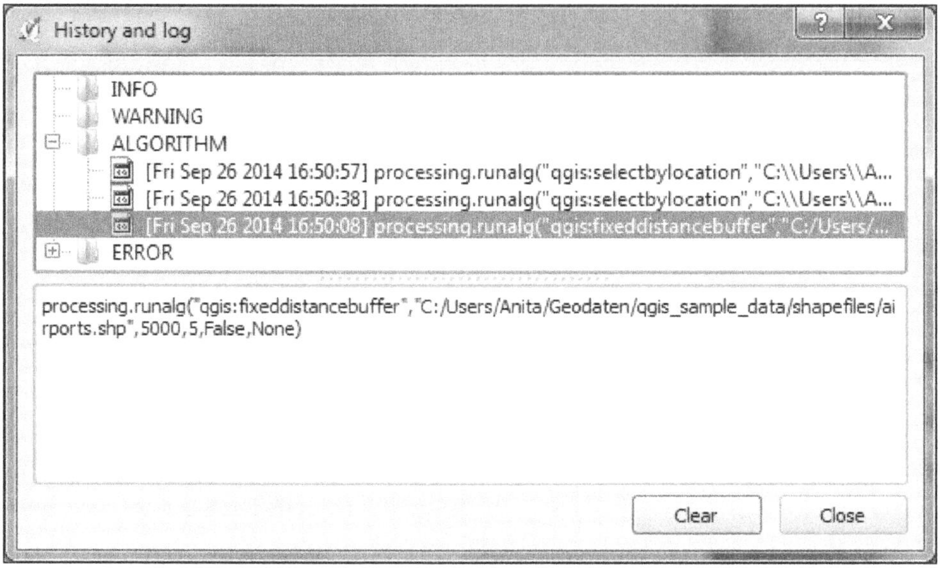

The commands listed under **ALGORITHM** can also be used to call Processing tools from the QGIS Python console by going to **Plugins** | **Python Console**. The Python commands shown in the following screenshot run the buffer algorithm (`processing.runalg`) and load the result into the map (`processing.load`):

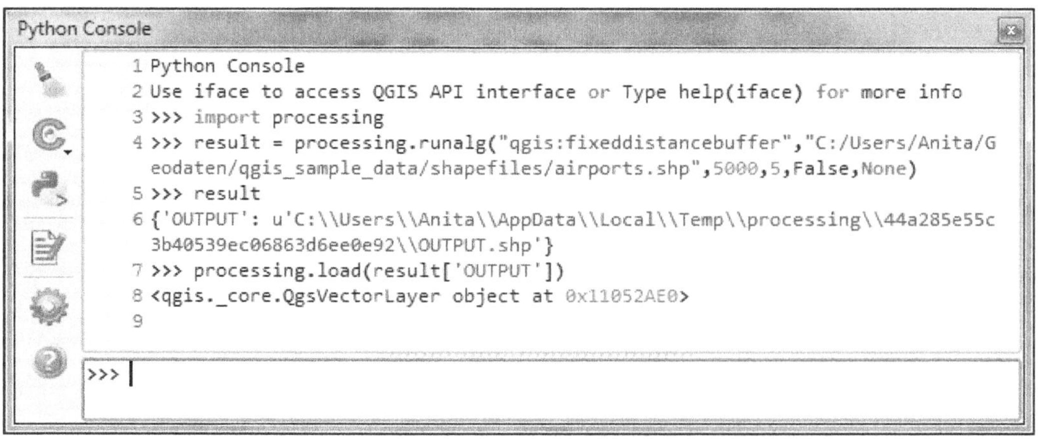

Raster sampling at point locations

Another common task is to sample a raster at specific point locations. Using Processing, we can solve this problem using a **GRASS** tool called `v.sample`. To use GRASS tools, make sure GRASS is installed and Processing is configured correctly by going to **Processing** | **Options and configuration**. On an OSGeo4W default system, the configuration will look like the following screenshot:

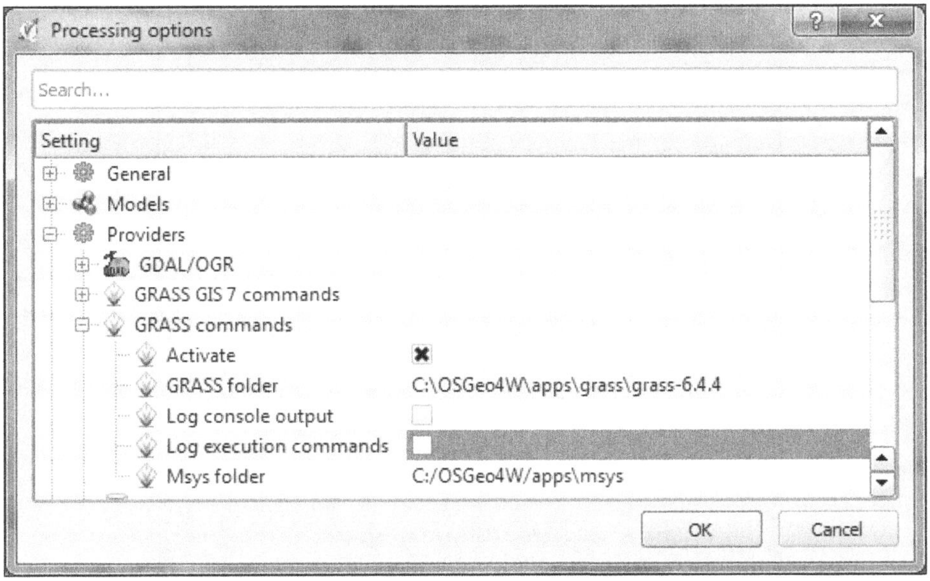

> At the time of writing this book, the current stable release is GRASS 6.4. As shown in the preceding screenshot, there is already a GRASS 7.0 beta release, and Processing can be configured to use its algorithms as well. In the toolbox, you will find the algorithms under **GRASS commands** and **GRASS GIS 7 commands**, respectively.

For this exercise, let's imagine that we want to sample the `landcover` layer at the airport locations of our sample data. All we have to do is specify the vector layer that contains the sample points and the raster layer that should be sampled. For this example, we can leave all the other settings to their defaults. The tool will not only sample the raster, it will also compare point attributes with the sampled raster value. However, we don't need this comparison in our current example. The dialog box will look like the following screenshot:

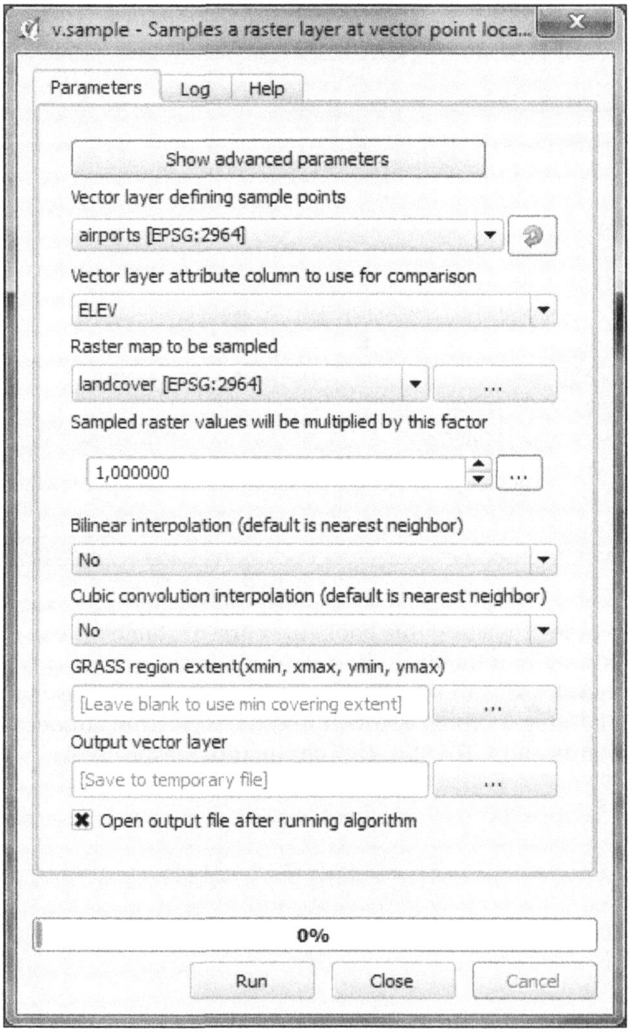

Mapping density with hexagonal grids

Mapping the density of points using a hexagonal grid has become a quite popular alternative to creating heatmaps. Processing offers us a fast way to create such an analysis. There is already a premade script called **Hex grid from layer bounds**, which we can use to first create a hexagonal grid that covers all the points in the input layer. The dataset of populated places, `popp.shp`, is a good sample dataset for this exercise. Once the grid is ready, we can run **Count points in polygon** to calculate the statistics. The number of points will be stored in the `NUMPOINTS` column if you use the settings shown in the following screenshot:

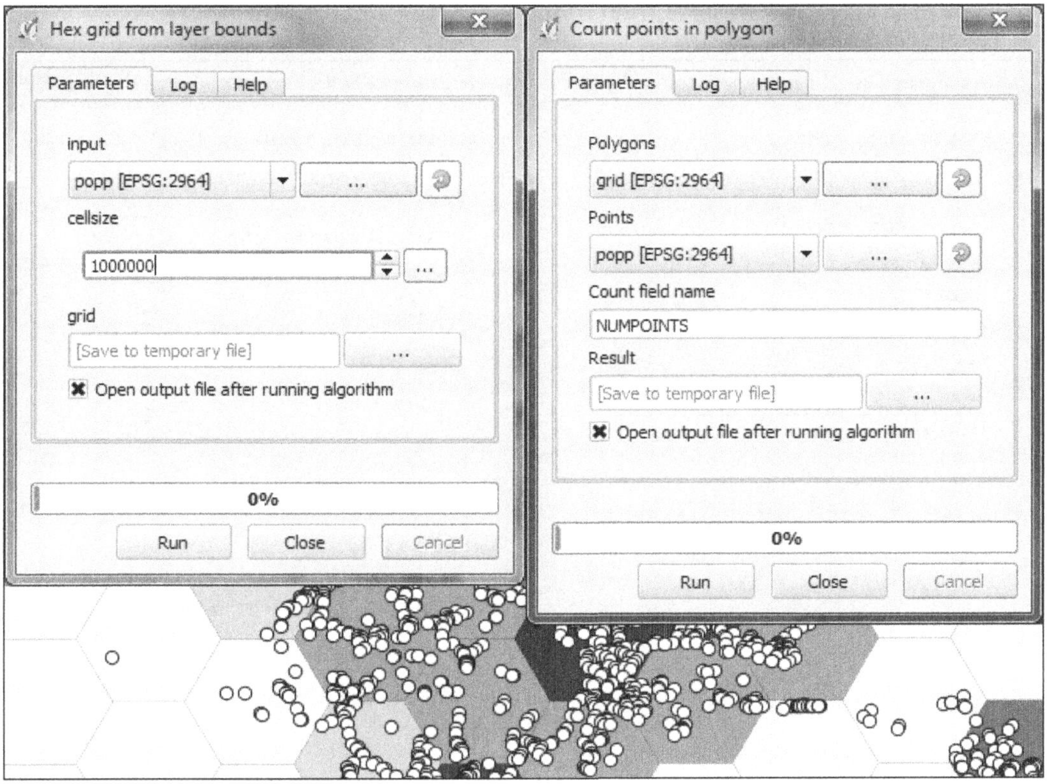

Calculating area shares within a region

Another spatial analysis task we often encounter is calculating area shares within a certain region, for example, land cover shares along one specific river. Using `majrivers.shp` and `trees.shp`, we can calculate the share of a wooded area in a 10,000-foot wide strip of land along the `Susitna River`. We will first define the analysis region by selecting the river and buffering it.

> QGIS Processing will only apply buffers to the selected features of the input layer. This default behavior can be changed by going to **Processing | Options and configuration** and disabling the **Use only selected features** option. For the following examples, leave the option enabled.

To select the Susitna river, we use the **Select by attribute** tool. After running the tool, you should see that the river lines are selected on the map. Then, we can use the **Fixed distance buffer** tool to get the area within 5,000 feet along the river. Note that the **Dissolve result** option should be set to **Yes** to ensure that the buffer result is one continuous polygon, as shown in the following screenshot:

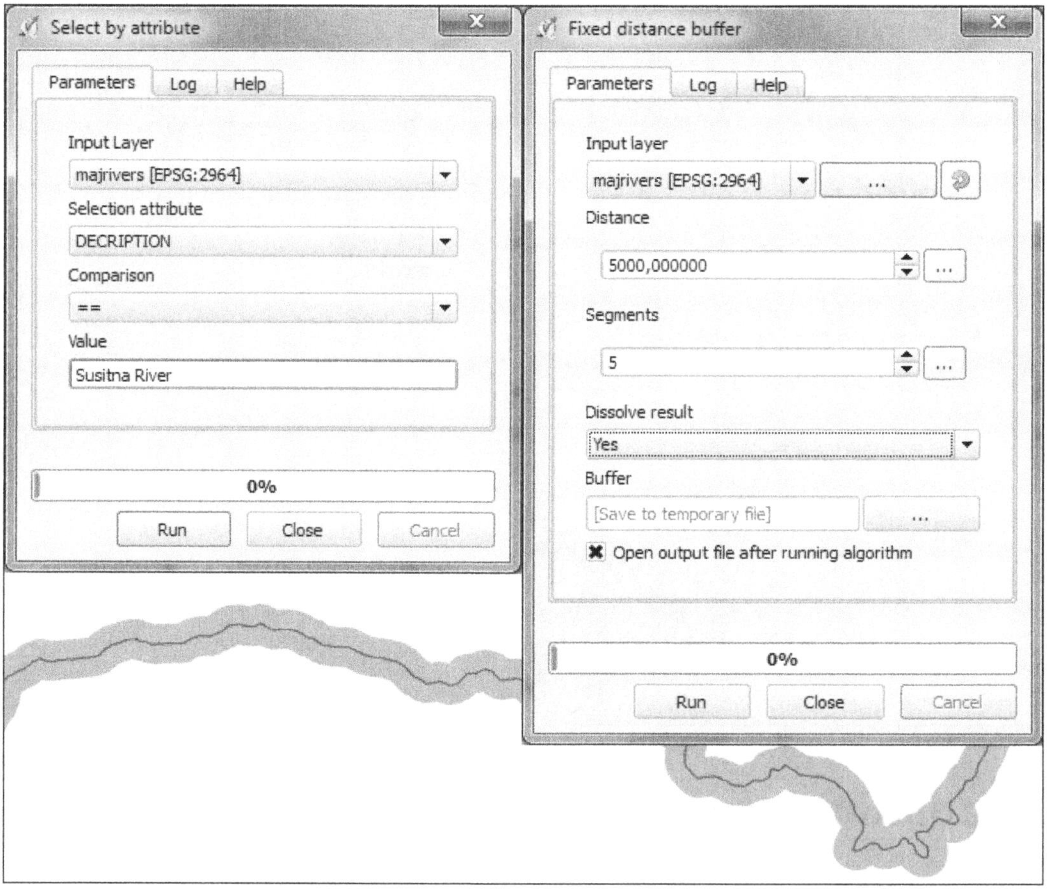

Next, we calculate the size of the strip of land around our river. This can be done using the **Export/Add geometry columns** tool, which adds the area and perimeter to the attribute table. Then, we can calculate the **Intersection** between the area along the river and the wooded areas in `trees.shp`, as shown in the following screenshot. The result of this operation is a layer that contains only those wooded areas that are within the river buffer.

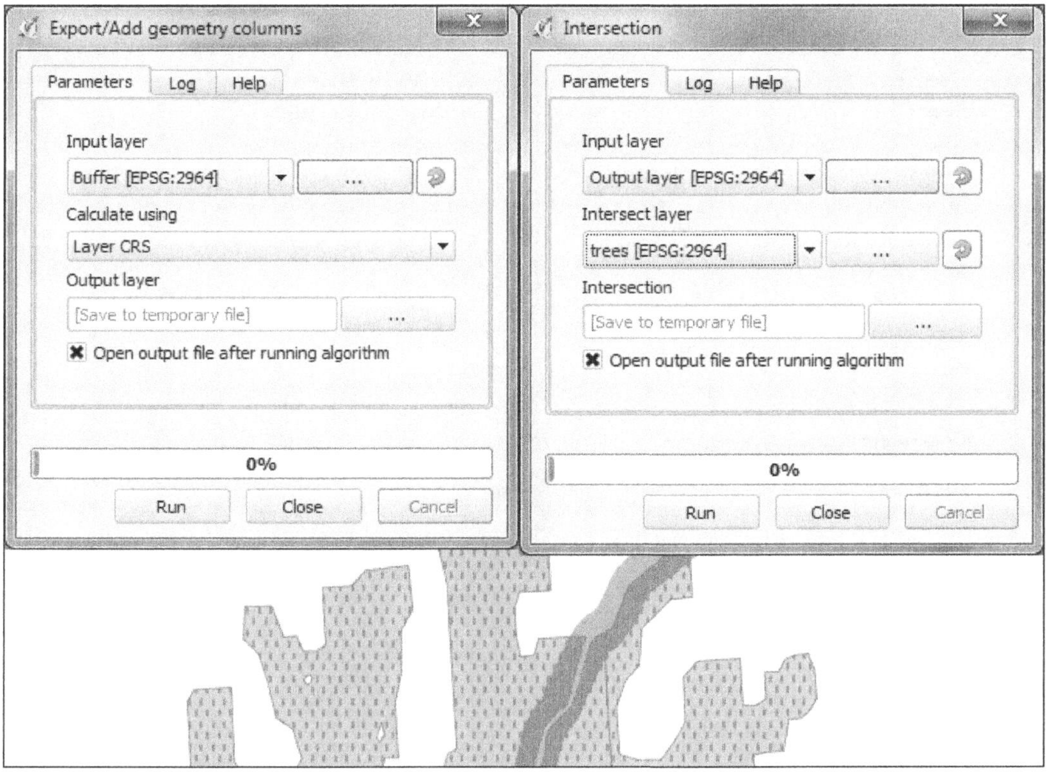

Using the **Dissolve** tool, we can recombine all the areas from the intersection results into one big polygon that represents the total wooded area around the river. Note how we use the unique ID field, `VEGDESC`, to only combine areas with the same vegetation so that we do not mix the deciduous and mixed trees.

Finally, we can calculate the final share of wooded area using **Advanced Python field calculator**. The `value = $geom.area()/<area>` formula divides the area of the final polygon (`$geom.area()`) by the value in the `area` attribute (`<area>`), which we created earlier by running **Export/Add geometry columns**. As shown in the following screenshot, this calculation results in a wood share of 0.31601 for **Deciduous** trees and 0.09666 for **Mixed** trees. Therefore, we can conclude that in total, 41.27 percent of the land along Susitna river is wooded.

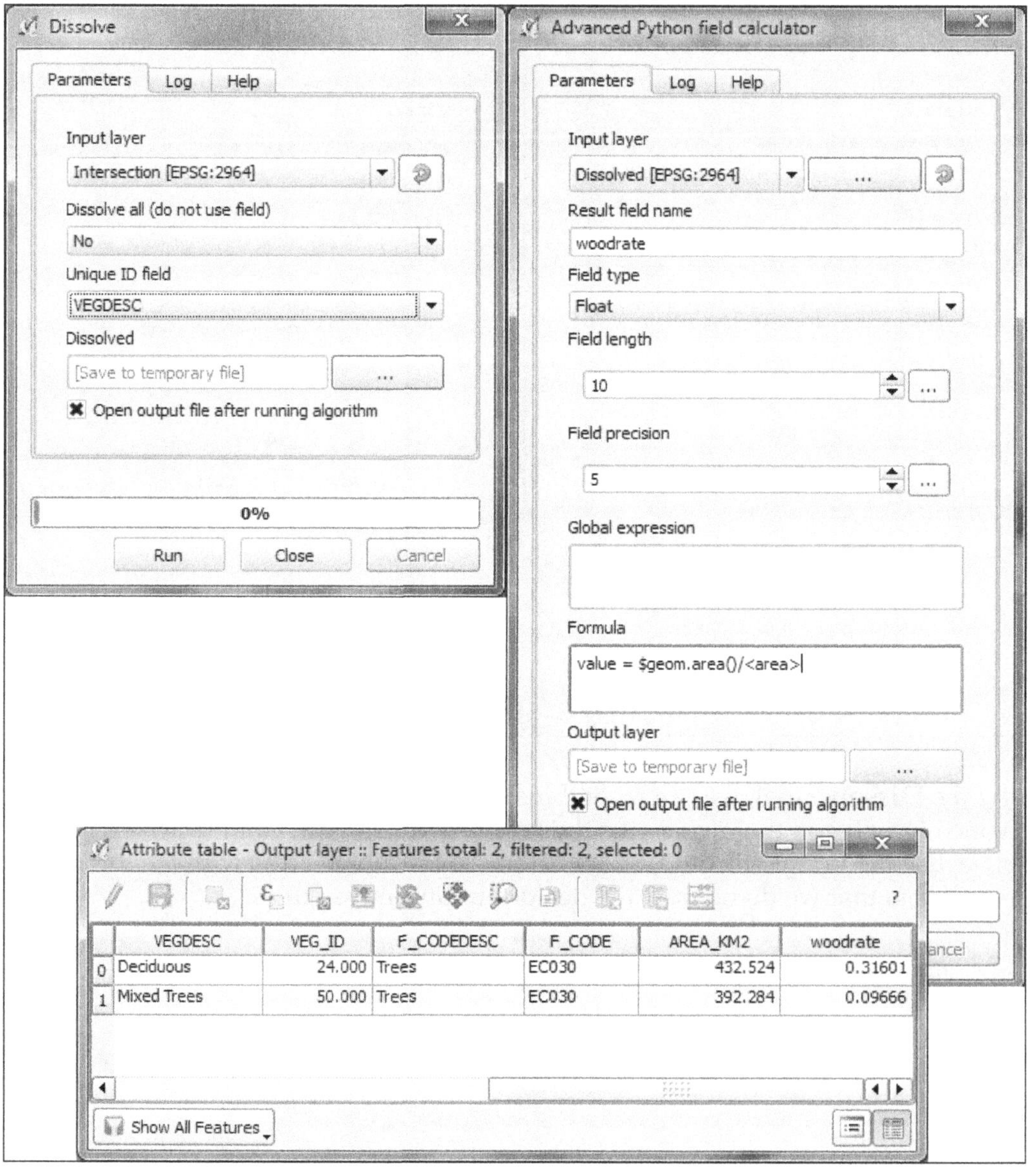

Automated geoprocessing with the graphical modeler

Using the graphical modeler, we can turn whole geoprocessing and analysis workflows into automated models; we can then use these models to run complex geoprocessing tasks that involve multiple different tools in one go. To create a model, we will go to **Processing** | **Graphical modeler** to open the modeler where we can select from different inputs and algorithms for our model.

Let's create a model that automates the creation of hexagonal heatmaps! By double-clicking on the **Vector layer** entry in the **Inputs** list, we can add an input field for the point layer. It's a good idea to use descriptive parameter names (for example, `hex cell size` instead of just `size` for the parameter that controls the size of the hexagonal grid cells) so that we can recognize which input is first and which is later in the model. It is also useful to restrict the **Shape type** field where appropriate. In our example, we will restrict the input to **Point**. This will enable Processing to prefilter the available layers and present us only with layers of the correct type. The second input we need is a **Number** field to specify the desired hexagonal cell size, as shown in the following screenshot:

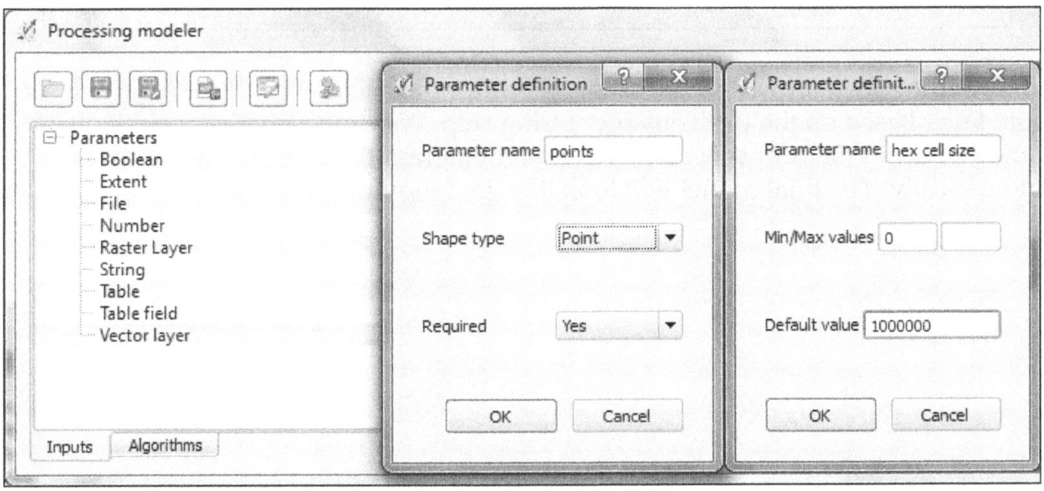

After adding the inputs, we can now continue creating the model by assembling the algorithms. In the **Algorithms** section, we can use the filter at the top to narrow down our search for the correct algorithm. To add an algorithm to the model, we will simply double-click on the entry in the list of algorithms. This opens the algorithm dialog box where we have to specify the inputs and further algorithm-specific parameters.

In our example, we want to use the point vector layer as the **input** layer and the number input **hex cell size** as the **cellsize** parameter. We can access the available inputs through the drop-down list, as shown in the following screenshot. Alternatively, it's also possible to hardcode parameters such as the cell size.

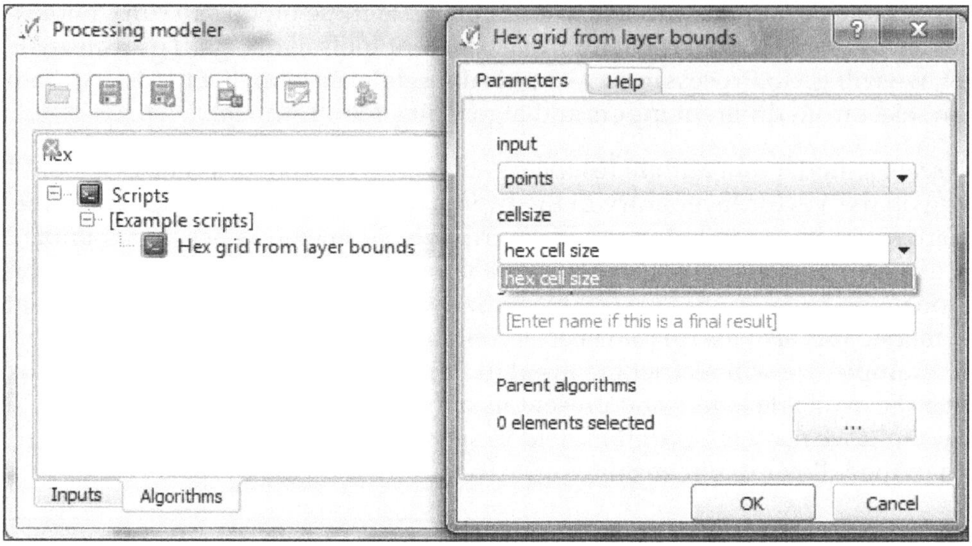

While adding the following algorithms, it is important to always choose the correct input layer based on the previous processing step. We can verify the correct workflow using the connections in the model diagram that the modeler draws automatically. The final model will look like the following screenshot:

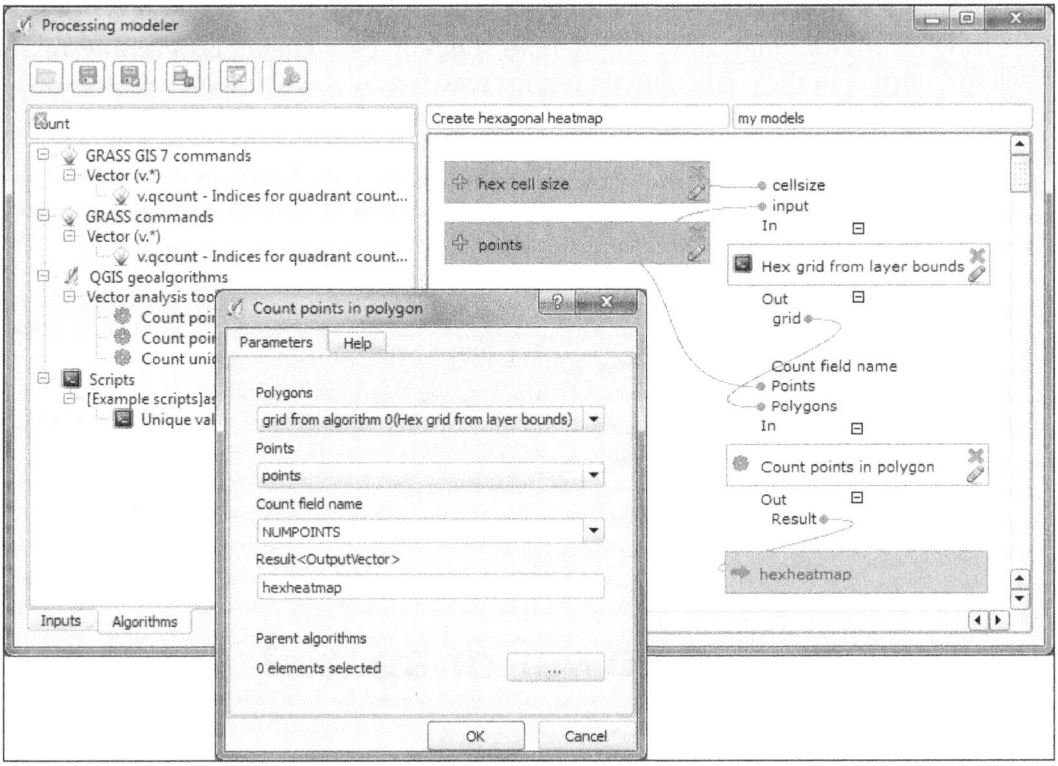

To finish the model, we should enter a model name (for example, `Create hexagonal heatmap`) and a group name (for example, `my models`). Processing will use the group name to organize all the models we create. Once we have picked a name and group, we can save the model and then run it. After closing the modeler, we can run the saved models from the toolbox like any other tool. It is even possible to use one model as a building block in another model.

Another useful feature is that we can specify a layer style to be applied to the processing results automatically. This default style can be set using **Edit rendering styles for outputs** in the context menu of the created model in the toolbox, as shown in the following screenshot:

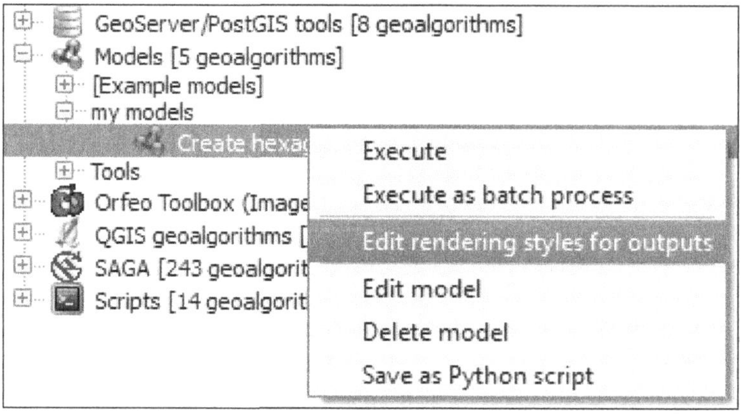

Leveraging the power of spatial databases

Another approach to geoprocessing is to use the functionality provided by spatial databases such as PostGIS or SpatiaLite. In the *Loading data from databases* section of *Chapter 2, Viewing Spatial Data*, we already discussed how to load data from a SpatiaLite database. In this exercise, we will use SpatiaLite's built-in geoprocessing function to perform spatial analysis directly in the database and visualize the results in QGIS. We will use the same SpatiaLite database we already downloaded in *Chapter 2, Viewing Spatial Data*, from `www.gaia-gis.it/spatialite-2.3.1/test-2.3.zip` (4 MB).

As an example, we will use SpatiaLite's spatial functions to get all the highways that are within 1 km distance of the city of Firenze. To interact with the database, we will use the **DB Manager** plugin; we can enable this plugin in **Plugin Manager**, and it is available via the **Database** menu. If you followed the *Loading data from databases* section of *Chapter 2, Viewing Spatial Data*, you will see `test-2.3.sqlite` listed under SpatiaLite in the tree on the left-hand side of the DB Manager dialog box, as shown in the following screenshot. If the database is not listed, please refer to the exercise mentioned earlier to set up the database connection.

Next, we will open the **SQL window** using the corresponding toolbar button by going to **Database | SQL window** or by pressing *F2*. The following SQL query will select all the highways that are within 1 km distance of the city of Firenze:

```
SELECT *
FROM HighWays
WHERE PtDistWithin(
  HighWays.Geometry,
  (SELECT Geometry FROM Towns WHERE Name = 'Firenze'),
  1000
)
```

The `SELECT Geometry FROM Towns WHERE Name = 'Firenze'` subquery selects the point geometry that represents the city of Firenze. This point is used in the `PtDistWithin` function to test for each highway geometry if it is within a distance of 1,000 meters.

> An introduction to SQL is out of the scope of this book, but you can find a full tutorial on using SpatiaLite at `http://www.gaia-gis.it/gaia-sins/spatialite-cookbook/index.html`. Additionally, to get an overview of all the spatial functionality offered by SpatiaLite, visit `http://www.gaia-gis.it/gaia-sins/spatialite-sql-4.2.0.html`).

When the query is entered, we can click on **Execute (F5)** to run the query. The query results will be displayed in tabular form in the **Result** section below the SQL query input area, as shown in the following screenshot:

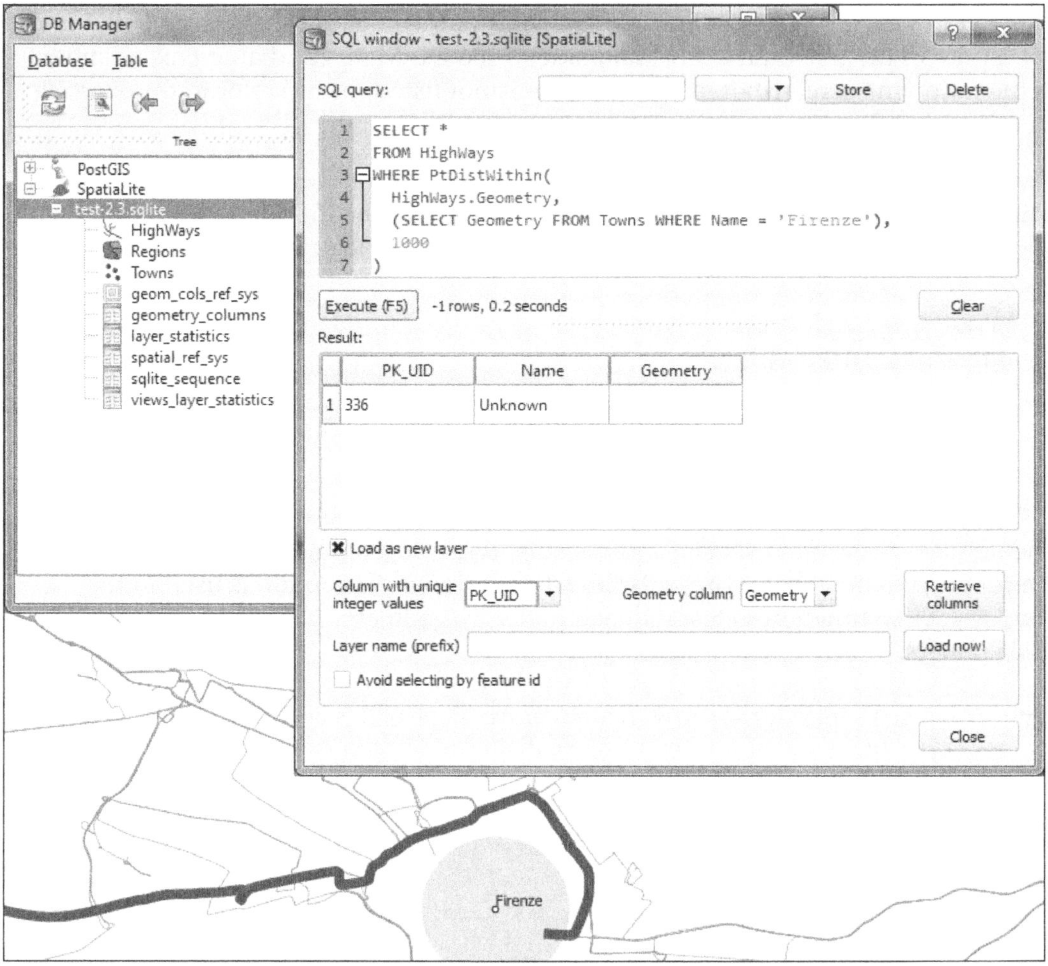

To display the query results on the map, we need to activate the **Load as new layer** option below the results table. Make sure that you select a suitable value for **Column with unique integer values** (`PK_UID` in our case) and **Geometry column** (`Geometry`). Once you have configured these settings, you can click on **Load now!** to load the query result as a new map layer. As you can see in the preceding screenshot, only one of the highways (represented by the wide blue line) is within 1 km of the city of Firenze.

> While we used SpatiaLite in this example, the tools and workflows presented in this chapter work just as well with PostGIS databases. It is worth noting though that SpatiaLite and PostGIS often use slightly different function names. Therefore, it is usually necessary to adjust the SQL queries accordingly.

Summary

In this chapter, we covered various raster and vector geoprocessing and analysis tools, and you learned how to apply them in common tasks. We saw how to use the Processing toolbox to run individual tools and we also saw how to use the modeler to create complex geoprocessing models from multiple tools. Using the modeler, we can automate our workflows and increase our productivity, especially with respect to reocurring tasks. Finally, we also took a quick look at how to leverage the power of spatial databases to perform spatial analysis.

In the following chapter, we will learn how to bring all skills learned so far together to create beautiful maps using advanced styles and print map composition features.

5
Creating Great Maps

In this chapter, we will cover the important features that enable us to create great maps. We will first go into advanced vector styling, building on what we learned in *Chapter 2, Viewing Spatial Data*. Then, you will learn how to label features by following examples for point labels as well as more advanced road labels with road shield graphics. We will also cover how to tweak labels manually. Finally, you will learn about the print composer and how to use it to create printable maps and map books. If you want to get an idea about what kind of maps you can create using QGIS, visit the QGIS Map Showcase Flickr group at `https://www.flickr.com/groups/qgis/`; this is dedicated to maps created with QGIS without any further postprocessing.

Advanced vector styling

This section introduces more advanced vector-styling features, building on the basics we saw in *Chapter 2, Viewing Spatial Data*. We will see how to create detailed custom visualizations using:

- Graduated styles
- Categorized styles
- Rule-based styles
- Data-defined styles

Creating a graduated style with size scaling

Graduated styles are great to visualize distributions of numeric values in a choropleth or a similar map. In our sample data, there is a `climate.shp` file; this contains locations and mean temperature values that we can visualize using a graduated style by simply selecting the **T_F_MEAN** value for the **Column** field and clicking on **Classify**. We can pick an existing color ramp or create a new one by scrolling down the list to the **New color ramp...** entry. Additionally, we can reverse the order of the colors within a **color ramp** using the **Invert** option.

Graduated styles are available in different classification modes as follows:

- **Equal Intervals**: This mode creates classes by splitting them at equal intervals between the maximum and minimum values found in the specified column.
- **Quantile (Equal Count)**: This mode creates classes so that each class contains an equal number of features.
- **Natural Breaks (Jenks)**: This mode uses the Jenks Natural Breaks algorithm to create classes by reducing the variance within classes and maximizing the variance between classes.
- **Standard Deviation**: This mode uses the column values' standard deviation to create classes.
- **Pretty Breaks**: This mode is the only classification that doesn't strictly create the specified number of classes. Instead, its main goal is to create class boundaries that are round numbers.

Besides using color to distinguish between the different temperature values, we can also use size. By setting **Size scale field** in the **Advanced** settings to **T_F_MEAN**, as shown in the following screenshot, all the point symbols will be scaled so that locations with higher mean temperatures are displayed with a bigger symbol.

> Using **Size scale field**, we can make the size of point symbols or the width of line symbols responsive to a certain attribute value. Note that we can choose between scaling the area or the diameter of a point symbol depending on the nature of the values. Similarly, there is also a **Rotation field** option, which allows us to rotate point symbols. The expected input is in degrees from 0 to 360, with 0 pointing towards the north.

Besides the symbols that are drawn on the map, another important aspect of the styling is the **legend** that goes with it. To customize the legend, we can define the **Label format** as well as the number of decimal places that should be displayed. In the **Label Format** string, `%1` will be replaced by the lower limit of the class, and `%2` will be replaced by the upper limit. You can change this string to suit your needs, for example, from `%1` to `%2`. If you activate the **Trim** option, excess trailing zeros will be removed as well.

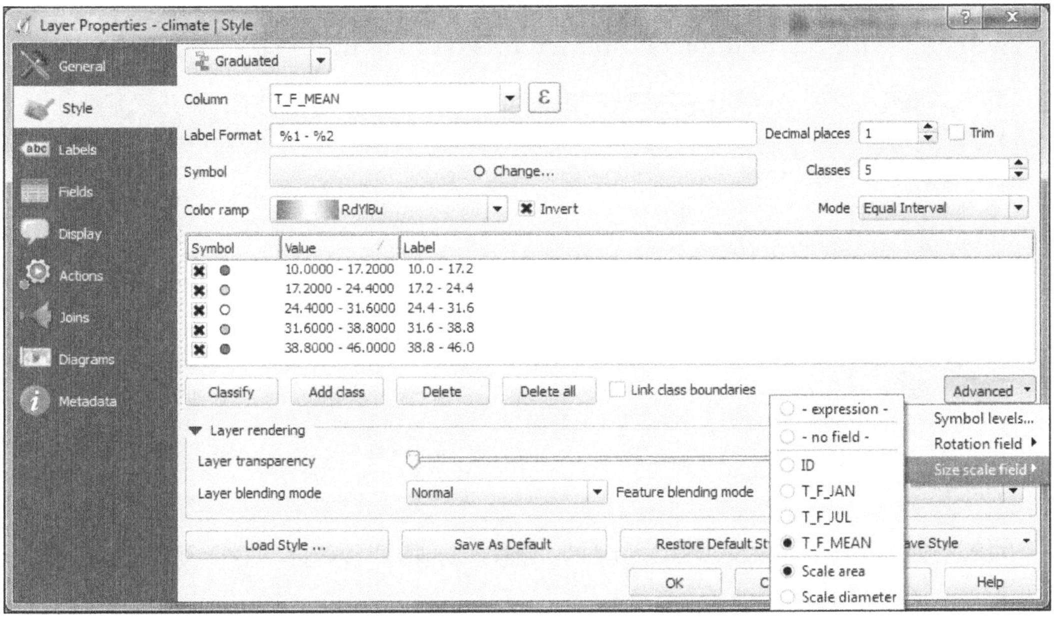

The following screenshot shows the results of using a **Graduated renderer** option, with five classes using the **Equal Interval** classification mode and a **Size scale field** option, as shown in the previous screenshot. Note the checkboxes beside each symbol; they can be used to selectively hide/show the features that belong to the corresponding class.

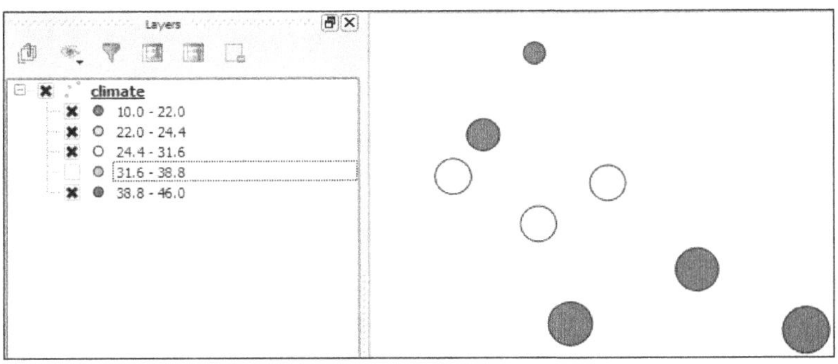

Using categorized styles

Just as graduated styles are very useful to visualize numeric values, categorized styles are great for text values or, more generally speaking, for all kinds of values on a nominal scale. A good example of this kind of data can be found in the `trees.shp` file in our sample data. For each area, there is a **VEGDESC** value that describes the type of forest found there. Using a categorized style, we can easily generate a style with one symbol for every unique value in the **VEGDESC** column, as shown in the following screenshot. Once we click on **OK**, the style is applied to our **trees** layer, and we can see the distribution of different tree types in the area.

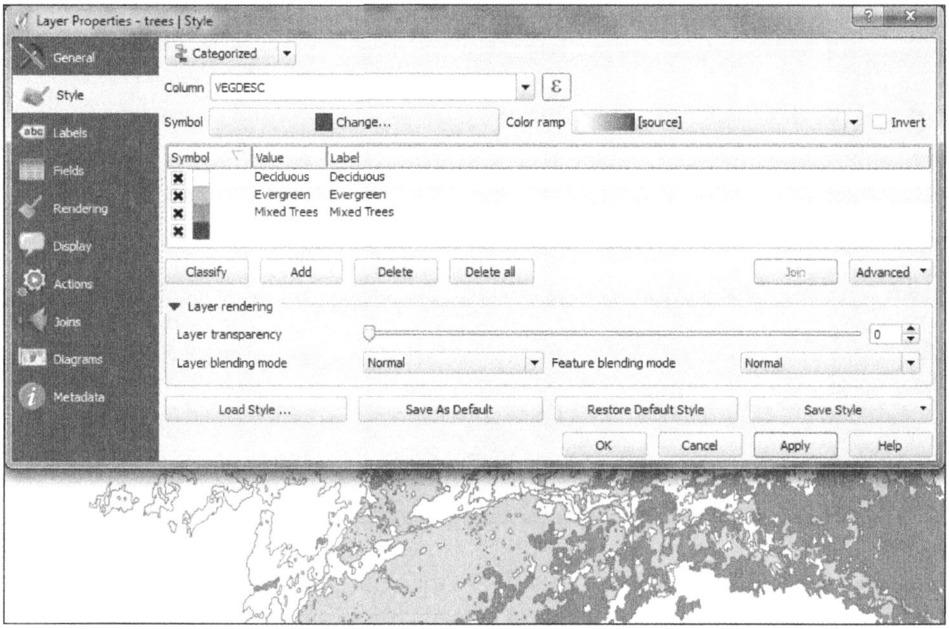

Of course, every symbol is editable and can be customized. Just double-click on the symbol preview to open the **Symbol** selector dialog, which allows us to select and combine different symbols.

Creating a rule-based style for road layers

With rule-based styles, we can create a layer style with a hierarchy of rules. Rules can take anything into account, from attribute values to scale and geometry properties such as area or length. In this example, we will create a rule-based renderer for the `ne_10m_roads.shp` file from **Natural Earth** (you can download it from `http://www.naturalearthdata.com/downloads/10m-cultural-vectors/roads/`). As you can see in the following screenshot, our style will contain different road styles for major and secondary highways; it will also contain scale-dependent styles:

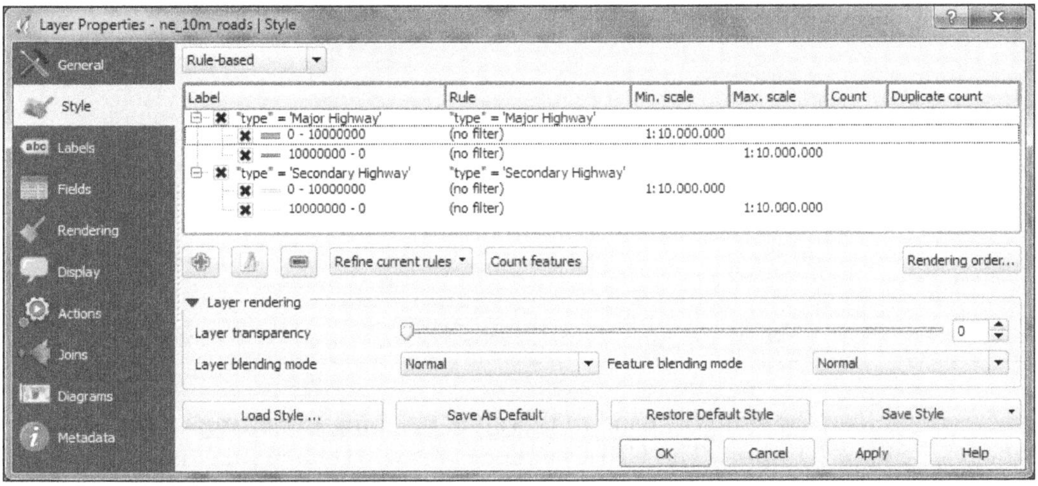

As you can see in the preceding screenshot, at the first level of rules, we distinguished between the roads of **"type" = 'Major Highway'** and those of **"type" = 'Secondary Highway'**. The next level of rules handles scale dependence. To add this second layer of rules, we can use the **Refine current rules** button and select **Add scales to rule**. We simply input one or more scale values at which we want the rule to be split.

> Note that there are no symbols specified at the first rule level. If we have symbols specified at the first level, the renderer would draw two symbols over each other. While this can be useful in certain cases, we don't want this effect now. Symbols can be deactivated in the **Rule** properties, which can be accessed by double-clicking on the rule or clicking on the edit button below the rule's tree view (the button between the plus and minus buttons).

In the following screenshot, we can see the rule-based renderer and the scale rules in action. While the left-hand side shows wider, white roads with gray outlines for secondary highways, the right-hand side shows a simplified version with thin grey lines.

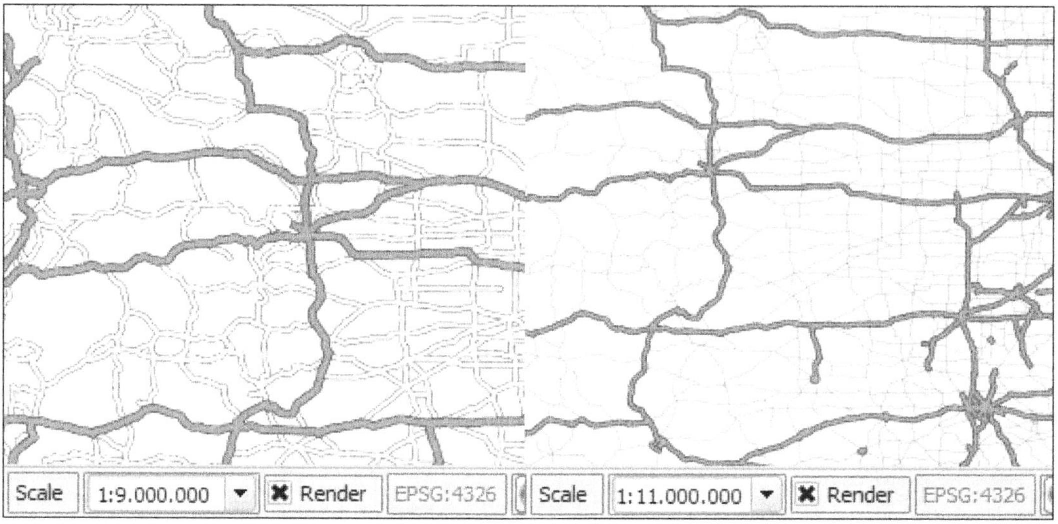

You can download the symbols used in this style by going to **Settings** | **Style Manager** | **Share** | **Import**. The URL is `https://raw.githubusercontent.com/anitagraser/QGIS-resources/master/qgis1.8/symbols/osm_symbols.xml`. Paste the URL in the **Location** textbox and click on **Fetch Symbols**, then on **Select all**, and finally on **Import**. The dialog will look like the following screenshot:

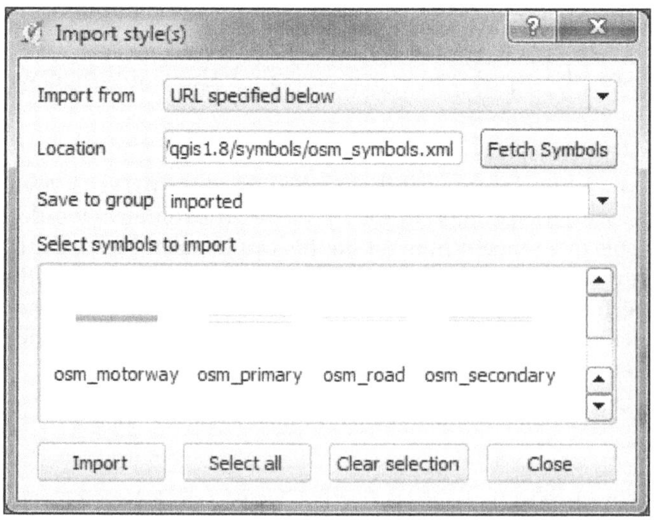

Creating data-defined symbology

In the previous section, *Creating a graduated style with size scaling*, we already used a simple form of data-defined symbology when we applied the size-scale field. However, there is much more we can do. In each symbol layer's properties, we find a **Data defined properties** button.

In this example, we will again use the `ne_10m_roads.shp` file from Natural Earth. The following screenshot shows the **Data defined properties** dialog of a simple line symbol layer. The available properties depend on the selected symbol layer type.

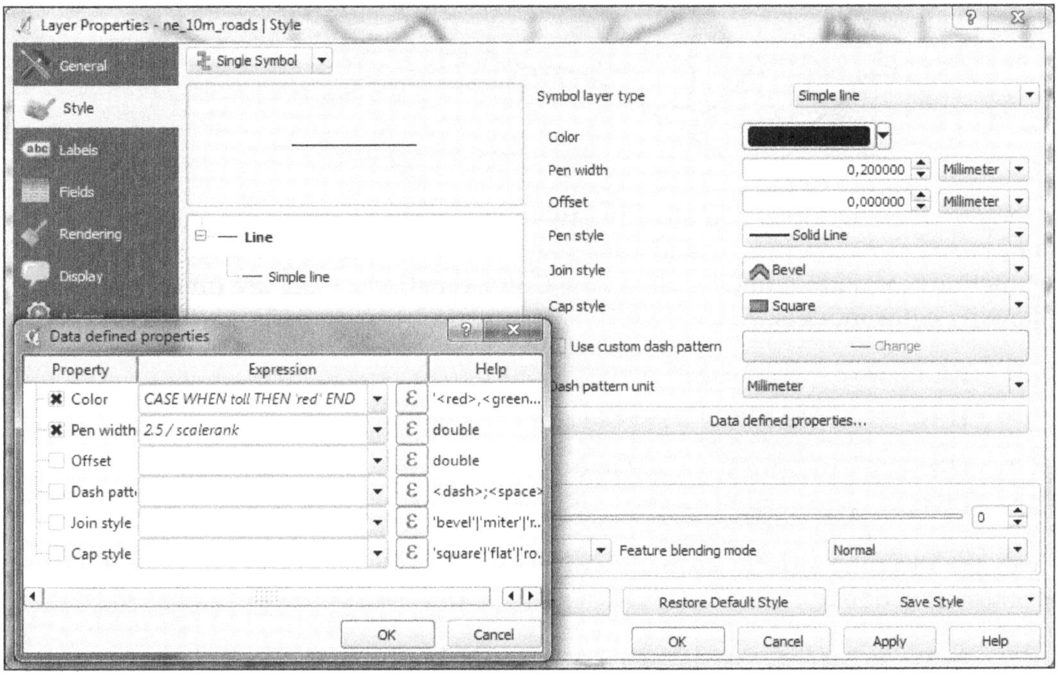

The configuration depicted in the previous screenshot creates a style where the line's **Pen width** depends on the feature's `scalerank`, and the line **Color** depends on the `toll` attribute. Let's look at the expressions more closely:

- `CASE WHEN toll THEN 'red' END`: This evaluates the `toll` value. If it is zero, the default color is unchanged—and therefore, black—but if the value is not zero (this means the feature is a toll road), the color is changed to red.
- `2.5 / scalerank`: This computes the **Pen width**. Since a low-scale rank should be represented by a wider line, we use a division operation instead of multiplication.

This is how the style looks:

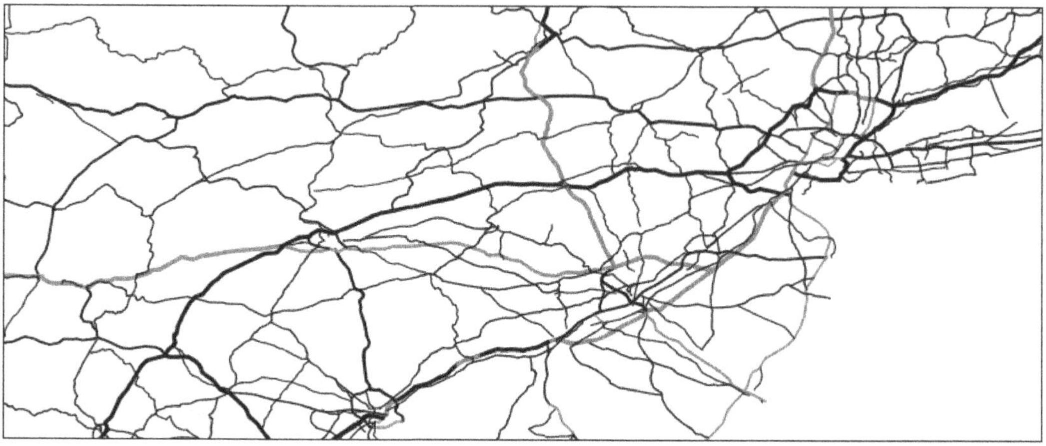

In the previous example, you already saw that you can specify colors using **color names** such as `'red'`, `'gold'` and `'deepskyblue'`. Another especially useful group of functions for data-defined styles is the **Color** functions; there are functions for the following **color models**:

- **RGB**: `color_rgb(red, green, blue)`
- **HSL**: `color_hsl(hue, saturation, lightness)`
- **HSV**: `color_hsv(hue, saturation, value)`
- **CMYK**: `color_cmyk(cyan, magenta, yellow, black)`

There are also functions to access the color ramps. Here are two examples of how to use these functions:

- `ramp_color('Reds', T_F_MEAN / 46)`: This returns a color from the `Reds` color ramp, depending on the `T_F_MEAN` value. Since the second parameter has to be a value between 0 and 1, we divide the `T_F_MEAN` value by the maximum value, which is `46`.

> Since users can add new color ramps or change the existing ones, the color ramps can vary between different QGIS installations. Therefore, the `ramp_color` function might return different results if the style or project file is used on a different computer.

- `color_rgba(0, 0, 180, scale_linear(T_F_JUL - T_F_JAN, 20, 70, 0, 255))`: This computes the color depending on the difference between the July and January temperatures, `T_F_JUL - T_F_JAN`. The difference value is transformed into a value between 0 and 255 by the `scale_linear` function according to the rule that says any value up to 20 will be translated to 0, any value of 70 and above will be translated to 255, and anything in between will be interpolated linearly. Bigger difference values result in darker colors because of the higher alpha-parameter value.

> The alpha component in `RGBA`, `HSLA`, `HSVA`, and `CMYKA` controls the transparency of the color. It can take on an integer value from 0 (completely transparent) to 255 (opaque).

Labeling

We can activate labeling by going to **Layer Properties** | **Labels**, checking the **Label this layer with** box, and selecting the attribute field that we want to use for the labels. This is all we need to do to display labels with default settings. While default labels are great for a quick preview, we would usually want to customize the labels if we create visualizations for reports or standalone maps.

Using **Expressions** (the button that is right beside the attribute drop-down list), we can format the label text to suit our needs. For example, the **NAME** field in our sample `airports.shp` file contains text in uppercase. To display the airport names in mixed case instead, we can set the `title(NAME)` expression; this will reformat the name text in title case. We can also use multiple fields to create the label, for example, combining name and elevation in brackets using the concatenation operator, `||`, as follows:

```
title(NAME) || ' (' || "ELEV" || ')'
```

Note the use of simple quotation marks around text, such as `' ('`, and double quotation marks around field names, such as `"ELEV"`. The dialog will look like the following screenshot:.

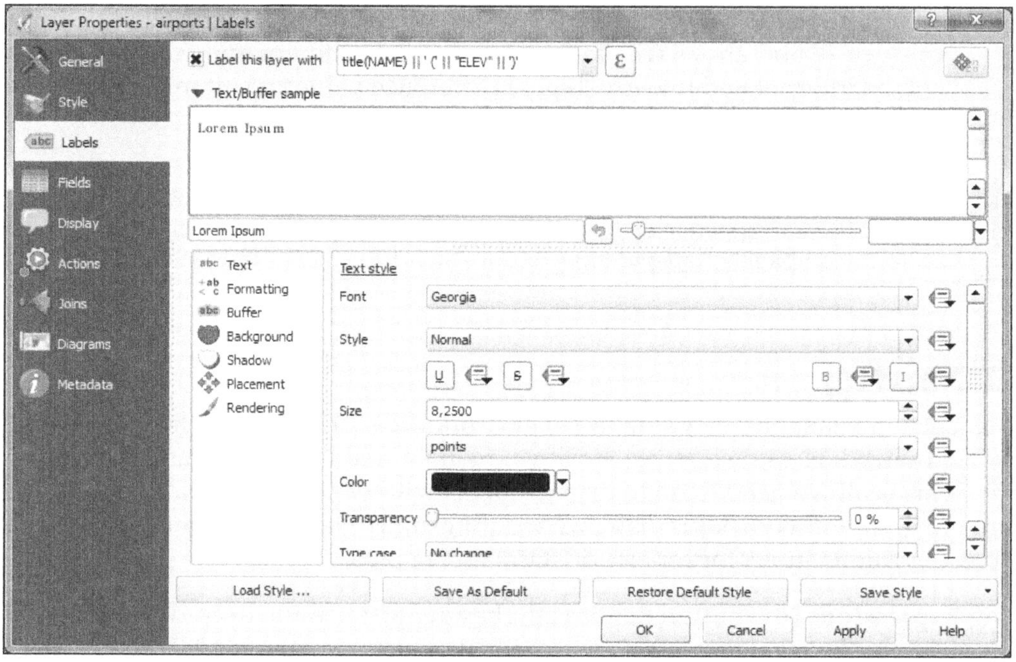

The big preview area titled **Text/Buffer sample** at the top of the dialog shows a preview of the current settings. The background color can be adjusted to test readability on different backgrounds. Under the preview area, we find the following label settings:

- **Text**: Besides changing the font style, size, color, and transparency, we can also modify **letter spacing** and **word spacing** as well as the blend mode, which works like the layer-blending mode we covered in *Chapter 2, Viewing Spatial Data*. Note the column of buttons on the right-hand side of every setting. Clicking on these buttons will allow us to create the so-called data-defined overrides. These can be used, for example, to define different label colors or change the label size depending on an individual feature's attribute value or expression.

- **Formatting**: Here, we can enable **multiline labels** by specifying which characters to wrap around. Additionally, we can control **line height** and **alignment**. We can also add a symbol that displays the line's digitizing direction to the label. Finally, the **Formatted numbers** option offers a shortcut to format numeric values to a certain number of decimal places.

  An alternative to wrapping texts around a certain character is the `wordwrap` function that is available in expressions. It wraps the input string to a certain maximum or minimum number of characters. The following screenshot shows an example of wrapping a longer text to a maximum of 22 characters per line:

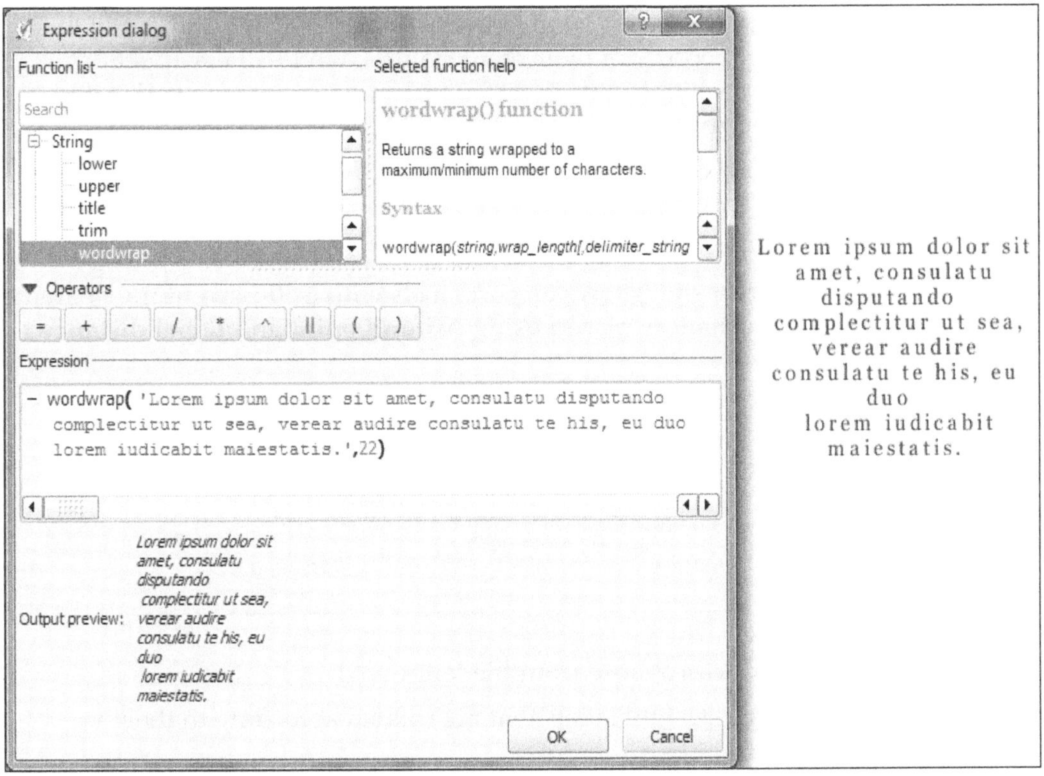

- **Buffer**: We can adjust the buffer size, color, and transparency, as well as the pen join style and blending mode. With transparency and blending, we can improve label readability without blocking out the underlying map too much.

- **Background**: This allows us to add a background shape in the form of a rectangle, square, circle, ellipsoid, or SVG. SVG backgrounds are great to create effects such as **highway shields**.
- **Shadow**: This makes it possible to add a shadow to labels. We can control everything from shadow direction to color, blur, size, and transparency.
- **Placement**: The available automatic label-placement options depend on the layer geometry type.

  For **point layers**, we can choose between the following:

  - The flexible **Around point** option tries to find the best position for labels by distributing them around the points without overlaps. As you can see in the following screenshot, some labels are put in the upper-right corner of their point symbol, while others appear at different positions in the left (for example, **Anchorage Intl (129)**) or lower-right (for example, **Bryant Ahp (345)**) corner.
  - The **Offset from point** option forces all the labels to a certain position; for example, all labels can be placed above their point symbols.

  The following screenshot shows airport labels with a 50-percent transparent **Buffer** and **Drop Shadow** placed using **Around point** and **Label distance** of 1 mm:

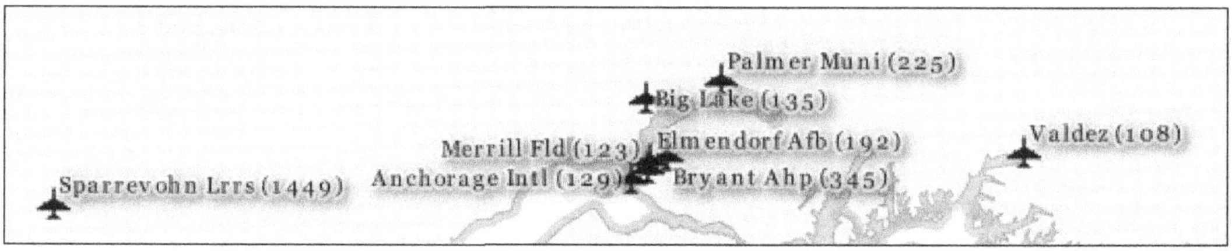

  For **line layers**, we can choose from the following:

  - **Parallel** for straight labels that are rotated according to the line orientation
  - **Curved** for labels that follow the shape of the line
  - **Horizontal** for labels that keep a horizontal orientation regardless of the line orientation

  For further fine-tuning, we can define whether the label should be placed as per one of these options: **Above line**, **On line**, or **Below line** and how far above and below using **Label distance**.

The following example shows labels with road shields. You can download a blank road-shield SVG from `http://upload.wikimedia.org/wikipedia/commons/c/c3/Blank_shield.svg`. Note how only Interstates are labeled. This can be achieved using the following labeling expression:

```
CASE WHEN "level" = 'Interstate' THEN name END
```

The labels are positioned using the **Horizontal** option. Additionally, **Merge connected lines to avoid duplicate labels** (in the **Rendering** section) and **Suppress labeling of features smaller than** are activated; for example, 5 mm helps avoid clutter by not labeling pieces of road that are shorter than 5 mm at the current scale.

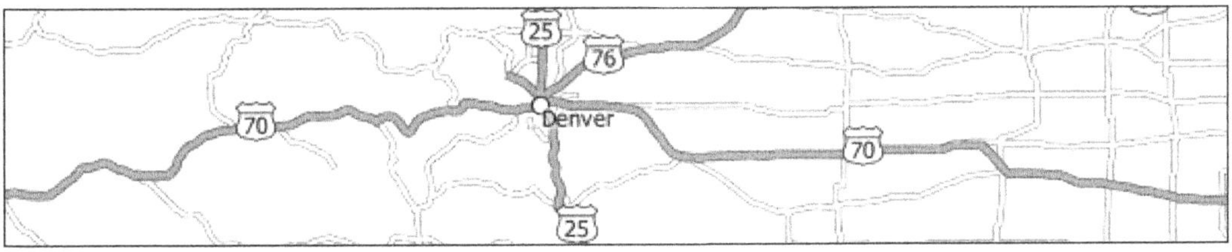

To set up the road shield, go to the **Background** section and select the blank-shield SVG from the folder you downloaded it to. To make sure that the label fits nicely inside the shield, we will additionally specify the **Size type** field as a buffer with a **Size** of 1 mm; this makes the shield a little bigger than the label it contains.

If you click on **Apply** now, you will notice that the labels are not centered perfectly inside the shields. To fix this, we will apply a small **Offset** in the **Y** direction to the shield position, as shown in the following screenshot. Additionally, it is recommended that you deactivate the **Buffer** label, as it tends to block out parts of the shield, and we don't need it anyway.

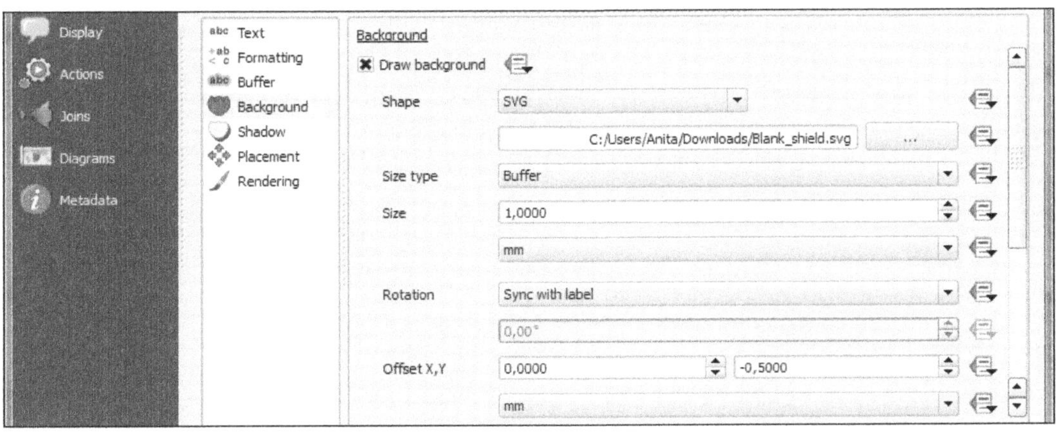

For **polygon layers**, the options are as follows:

- **Offset from centroid** uses the polygon centroid as an anchor and works like **Offset from point** for point layers
- **Around centroid** works in a manner similar to **Around point**
- **Horizontal** places a horizontal label somewhere inside the polygon, independent of the centroid
- **Free** fits a freely rotated label inside the polygon
- **Using perimeter** places the label on the polygon outline

- **Rendering**: This allows us to define scale-based visibility limits to display labels only on certain scales and pixel-size-based visibility to hide labels for small features. Here, we can also tell the labeling engine to show colliding labels, which are normally hidden by default.

> By default, QGIS avoids overlapping labels, but for debug purposes, it can be useful to force **Show all labels (including colliding labels)** using the options in the **Rendering** section.

The following screenshot shows lake labels (`lakes.shp`) using the **Multiple lines** feature wrapping on the empty space character, **Center Alignment**, a **Letter spacing** value of 2, and positioned using the **Free** option:

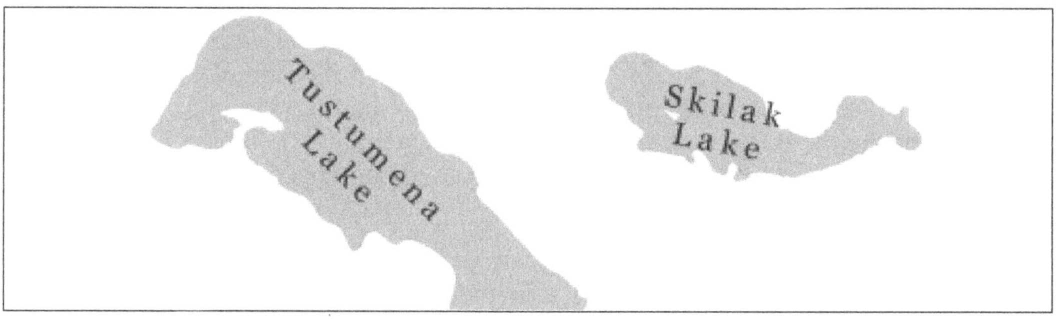

Besides automatic label placement, we also have the option to use data-defined placement to position labels exactly where we want them to be. In the labeling toolbar, we will find tools to move and rotate labels by hand. They are only active and available for layers that have data-defined placement set up for at least the X and Y coordinates. To start using the tools, we can simply add three new columns, `label_x`, `label_y`, and `label_rot` to, for example, the `airports.shp` file. Then, we can specify these columns in the data-defined settings by pressing the buttons beside **Offset X, Y,** and **Rotation**. We don't have to enter any values in the attribute table right now. The labeling engine will check for values, and if it finds the attribute fields empty, it will simply place the labels automatically. By specifying data-defined placement, the labeling toolbar's tools are now available (note that the editing mode has to be turned on), and we can use the tools to move and rotate any of the labels on the map. The changes are written back to the attribute table. Try moving some labels, especially where they are placed closely together, and watch how the automatically placed labels adapt to your changes.

Designing print maps

In QGIS, **print maps** are designed in the print composer. A QGIS project can contain multiple composers, so it makes sense to pick descriptive names. Compositions are saved automatically whenever we save the project. To see a list of all the compositions available in a project, go to **Project | Composer Manager**.

We can open a new composer by going to **Project | New Print Composer** or using *Ctrl + P*. The composer window consists of the following:

- A preview area for the map composition; this area displays a blank page at first
- Panels to configure **Composition**, **Item properties**, and **Atlas generation**, as well as a **Command history** panel for quick undo and redo actions
- Toolbars to manage, save, and export compositions, navigate in the preview area, as well as add and arrange different composer items

Once you have designed your print map the way you want it, you can save the template to a composer template `.qpt` file by navigating to **Composer | Save as template** and reuse it in other projects by navigating to **Composer | Add Items from Template**.

Creating a basic map

The **Composition** panel gives us access to the paper options such as size, orientation, and number of pages. It is also the place to configure snapping behavior and output resolution.

First, we add a map item to the paper using the **Add new map** button or by going to **Layout** | **Add Map** and drawing the map rectangle onto the paper. Click on the paper, keep the mouse button pressed down, and drag the rectangle open. We can move, and resize the map using the mouse and the **Select/Move item** tools. Alternatively, it is also possible to configure all the map settings in the **Item Properties** panel.

The **Item Properties** panel content depends on the currently selected composition item. If a map item is selected, we can adjust the map's **Scale** and **Extents** as well as the **Position and size** tool of the map item itself. At a **Scale** value of 10,000,000, we can more or less fit Alaska on an A4-size paper. To move the area that is displayed within the map item, and change the map scale we can use the **Move item content** tool.

After the map looks like we want it to, we can add a scale bar using the **Add new scalebar** button or by going to **Layout** | **Add Scalebar** and clicking on the map. The **Item Properties** panel now displays the scalebar's properties, which are similar to what you can see in the following screenshot. Since we can add multiple map items to one composition, it is important to specify which map the scale belongs to. The second main property is the scalebar style, which allows us to choose between different scalebar types or a **Numeric** type for a simple textual representation such as 1:10,000,000. Using the **Units** properties, we can convert the map units in feet or meters to something more manageable, such as miles or kilometers. The **Segments** properties control the number of segments and the size of a single segment in the scalebar. Furthermore, the properties control the scalebar's color, font, background, and so on.

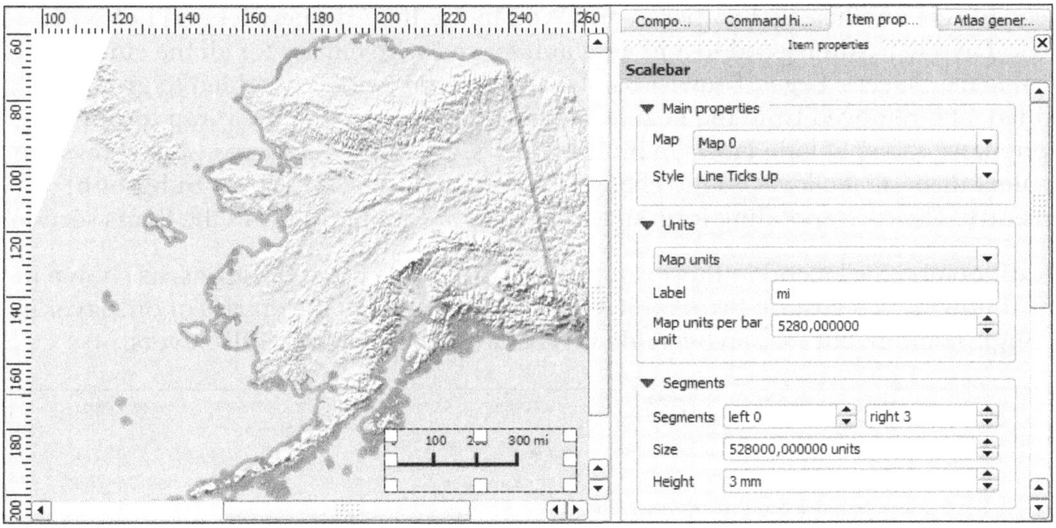

North arrows can be added to a composition using the **Add Image** button or by going to **Layout** | **Add image** and clicking on the paper. To use one of the SVGs, which are part of the QGIS installation, open the **Search directories** section in the **Item Properties** panel. It might take a while for QGIS to load the previews of the images in the SVG folder. You can pick a north arrow from the list of images or select your own image by clicking on the button next to the **Image source** input. More map decorations such as arrows or a rectangle, triangle, or ellipse shapes can be added using the appropriate toolbar buttons such as **Add Arrow**, **Add Rectangle**, and so on.

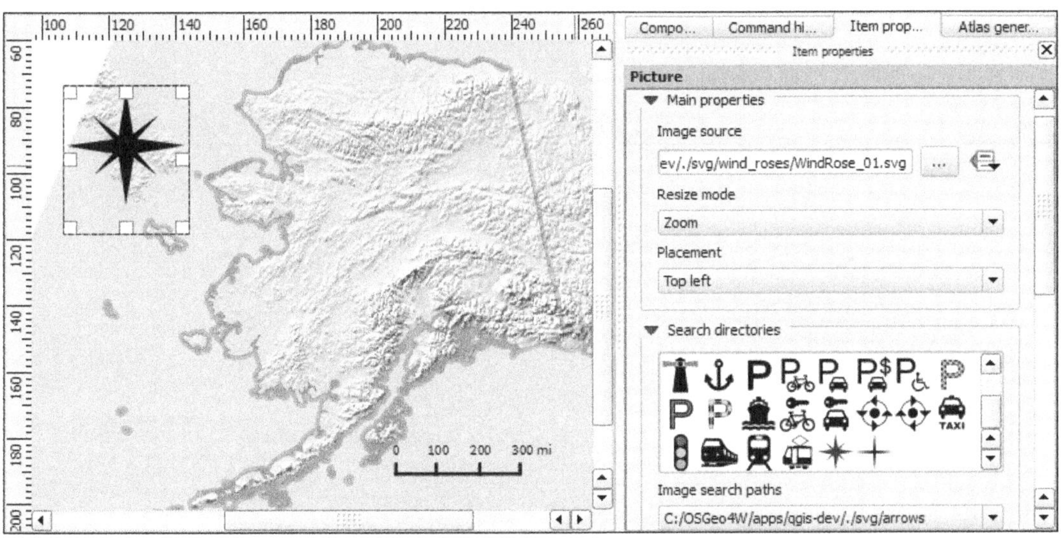

Legends are another vital map element. We can use the **Add new legend** button or go to **Layout** | **Add legend** to add a default legend with entries for all the currently visible map layers. Legend entries can be reorganized (sorted or added to groups), edited, and removed from the **Legend items**' properties. Using the **Wrap text on** option, we can split long labels in multiple rows. The following screenshot shows the context menu that allows you to change the style (**Hidden**, **Group**, or **Subgroup**) of an entry. The corresponding font, size, and color are configurable in the **Fonts** section.

Additionally, the legend in this example is divided into three **Columns**, as shown in the following screenshot. By default, QGIS tries to keep all the entries of one layer in a single column, but we can override this behavior be enabling **Split layers**.

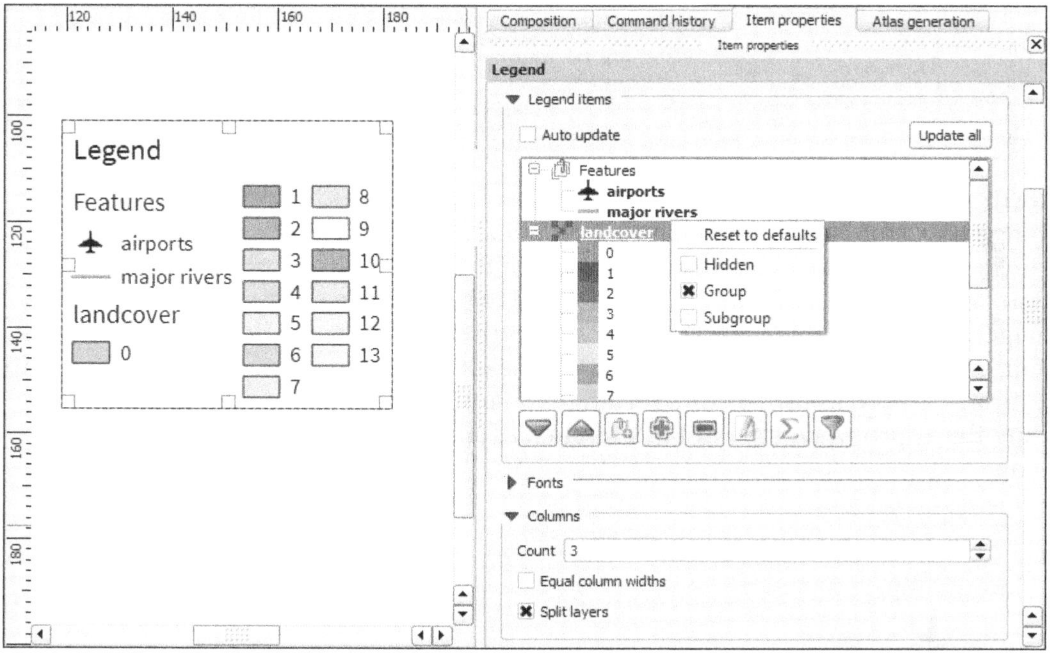

To add text to the map, we can use the **Add new label** button or go to **Layout | Add label**. Simple labels display all text using the same font. By enabling **Render** as HTML, we can create more elaborate labels with headers, lists, different colors, and highlights in bold or italics using the normal HTML notation, for example:

```
<h1>Alaska</h1><h1>Alaska</h1>
<p>The name <i>"Alaska"</i> means "the mainland".</p>
<ul><li>one list entry</li><li>another entry</li></ul>
<p style="font-size:70%;">[% format_date( $now ,'yyyy-mm-dd')%]</p>
```

Labels can also contain expressions such as the following:

- `[% $now %]`: This inserts the current timestamp, which can be formatted using the `format_date` function, as shown in the following screenshot
- `[% $page %] of [% $numpages %]`: This is used to insert page numbers in compositions with multiple pages

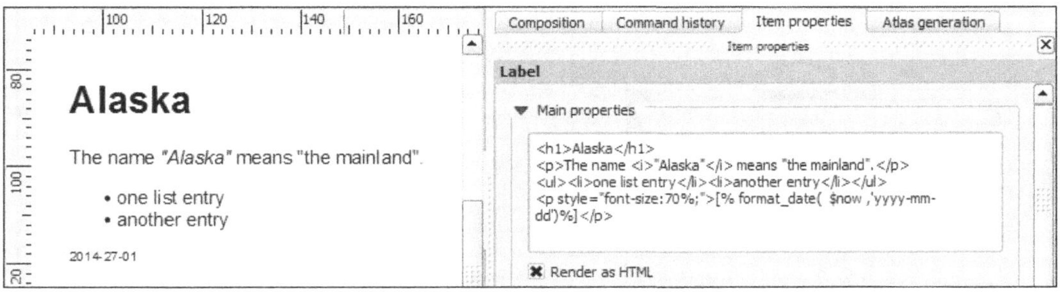

Adding advanced map items

Other common map features are **grids** and **frames**. Every map item can have one or more grids. Click on the **+** button in the **Grids** section to add a grid. The **Interval** and **Offset** values have to be specified in map units. We can choose between the following grid types:

- A normal **Solid** grid with customizable lines
- **Crosses** at the specified intervals with customizable styles
- Customizable **Markers** at the specified intervals
- **Frame and annotation only** will hide the grid while still displaying the frame and coordinate annotations

For **Grid frame**, we can select from the following frame styles:

- **Zebra** with customizable line and fill colors, as shown in the following screenshot
- **Interior ticks**, **Exterior ticks**, or **Interior and exterior ticks** for tick marks that point inside the map, outside, or in both the directions
- **Line border** for a simple line frame

Using **Draw coordinates**, we can label the grid with the corresponding coordinates. The labels can be aligned horizontally or vertically and placed inside or outside the frame, as shown in the following screenshot:

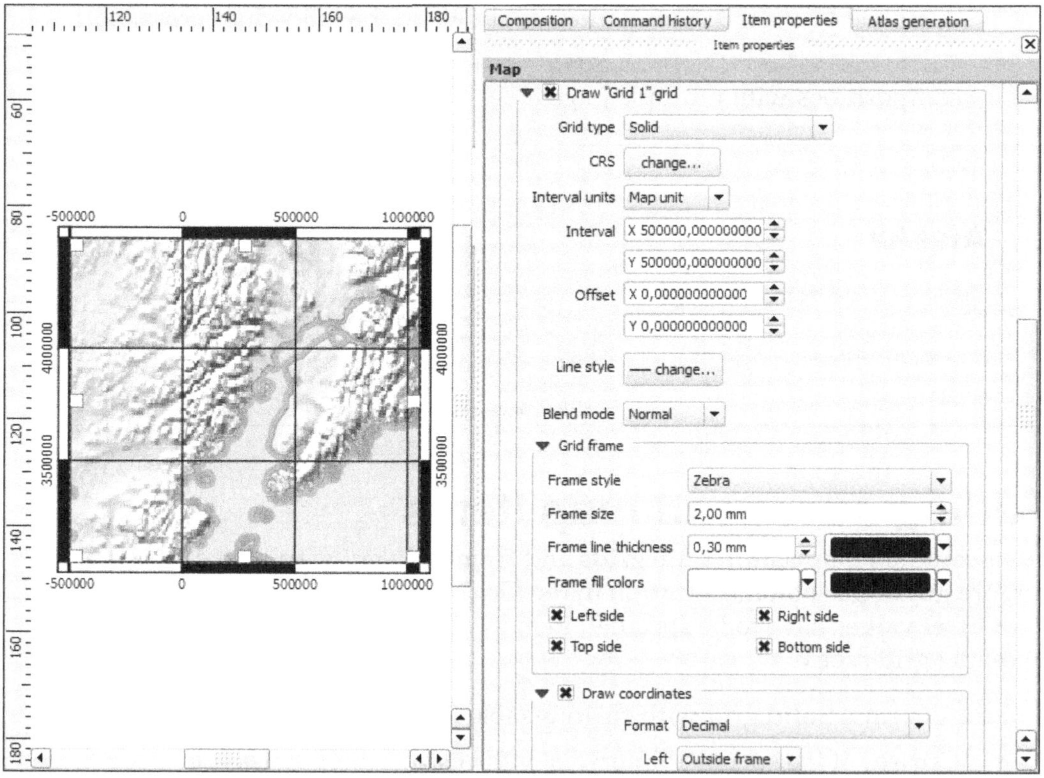

Maps that show an area close up are often accompanied by a second map that tells the reader where the area is located in a larger context. To create such an **overview map**, we will add a second map item and add an overview by clicking on the **+** button in the **Overviews** section. By setting **Map frame**, we can define which detail map's extent should be highlighted. By pressing the **+** button again, we can add additional map frames to the overview map. The following screenshot shows an example with two detail maps, both of which are added to an overview map. To distinguish between the two maps, the overview highlights are color-coded (by changing the overview's frame style) to match the colors of the frames of the detail maps.

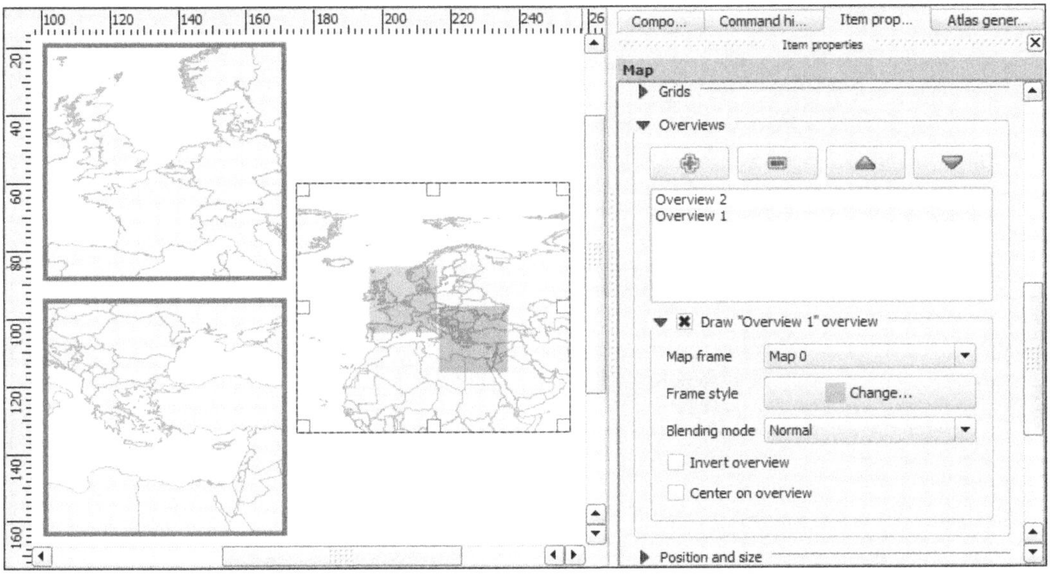

> Every map item in a composition can display a different combination of layers. Generally, map items in a composer are synced with the map in the main QGIS window. So, if we turn a layer off in the main window, it gets removed from the print composer map as well. However, we can stop this automatic synchronization by enabling **Lock layers** for a map item in the map item's properties.

To add additional details to the map, the composer also offers the possibility to add an attribute table to the composition using the **Add attribute table** button or by going to **Layout** | **Add attribute table**. By enabling **Show only features visible within a map**, we can filter the table and display only the relevant results. Additional filter expressions can be set using the **Filter with** option. Sorting (for example, by name, as shown in the following screenshot) and renaming of columns is possible via the **Attributes** button. The table-styling options can be accessed in the **Appearance** section to, for example, create a header line with bold and centered text.

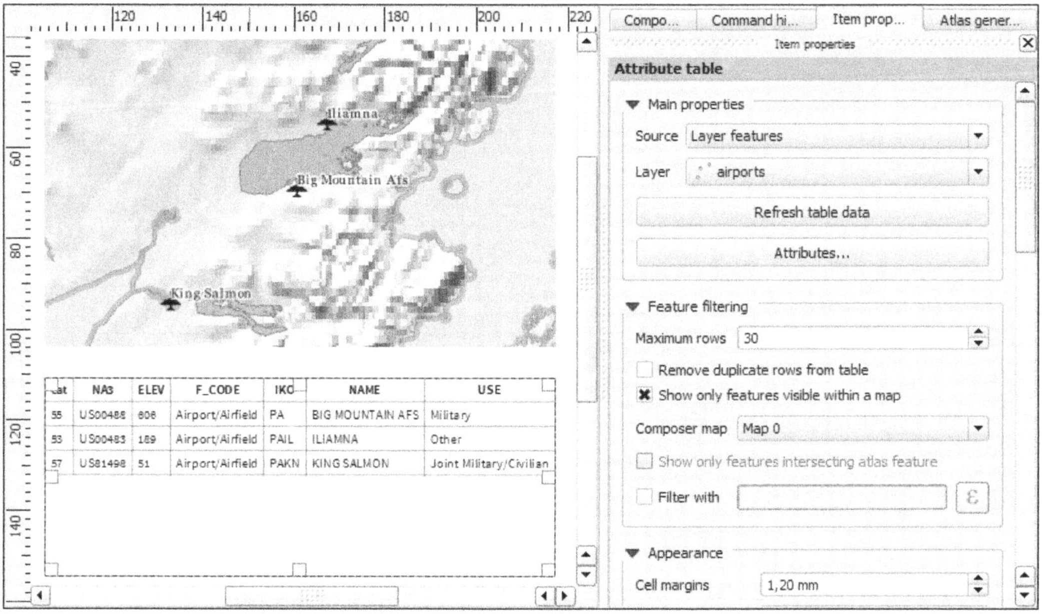

Even more advanced content can be added using the **Add html frame** button. We can point the item's URL reference to any HTML page on our local machines or online, and the content (text and images as displayed in a web browser) will be displayed on the composer page.

Creating map series using the Atlas feature

With the print composer's Atlas feature, we can create a series of maps using one print composition. The tool will create one output (can be image files, PDFs, or PDF pages) for every feature in the so-called **Coverage layer**.

Atlas can control and update multiple map items within one composition. To enable Atlas for a map item, we have to enable the **Controlled by atlas** option in the **Item properties** of the map item. Using the **Fixed scale** option in the **Controlled by atlas** section, all maps will be rendered using the same scale. If we need more flexible output, we can switch to the **Margin around feature** option instead, which zooms to every **Coverage** layer feature and renders it in addition to the specified margin-surrounding area.

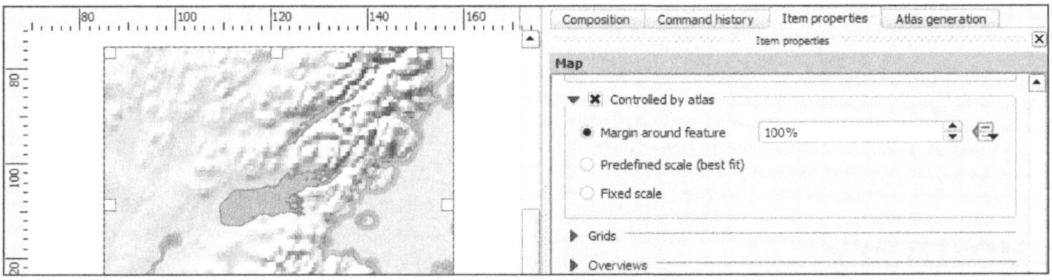

To finish the configuration, we will switch to the **Atlas generation** panel. As mentioned earlier, Atlas will create one map for every feature in the layer configured in the **Coverage layer** dropdown. Features in the **Coverage layer** can be displayed like regular features or can be hidden by enabling **Hidden coverage layer**. Adding an expression to the **Feature filtering** option or enabling the **Sort by** option makes it possible to further fine-tune the results. The **Output** field can be one image or PDF for each **Coverage layer** feature, or you can make it a multipage PDF by enabling **Single file export when possible**, before going to **Composer** | **Export as PDF**.

Once these configurations are set, we can preview the map series by enabling the preview atlas button, which you can see in the upper-left corner of the following screenshot. The arrow buttons next to the preview button are used to navigate between the Atlas maps.

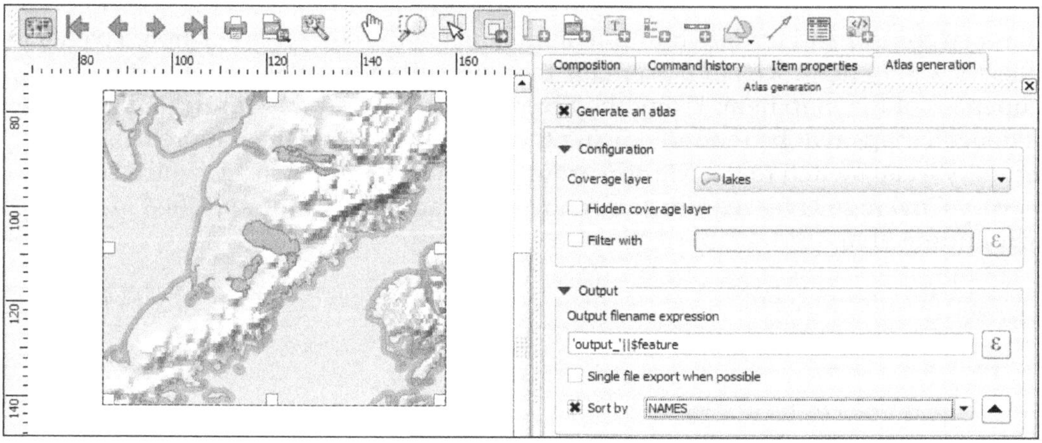

Summary

In this chapter, we had a closer look into how we can create some more complex maps using advanced vector-layer styles such as the categorized or rule-based style. We also covered the automatic and manual feature-labeling options available in QGIS. This chapter also showed you how to create printable maps using print composer, and it introduced the Atlas functionality to create map books. Congratulations! In the chapters so far, you learned how to install and use QGIS to create, edit, and analyze spatial data and how to present it in an effective manner. In the following chapter, we will have a look at expanding the QGIS functionality using Python.

6

Extending QGIS with Python

This chapter is an introduction to scripting QGIS with Python. Of course, a full-blown Python tutorial is out of the scope of this book. The examples here, therefore, assume a minimum proficiency when working with Python. Python is a very accessible programming language even if you are just getting started, and it has gained a lot of popularity in both the open source and proprietary GIS worlds, for example, ESRI's **ArcPy** or **PyQGIS**. QGIS currently supports Python 2.7, and at the time of writing this book, there is no Python 3 support. We will start with an introduction to the QGIS Python console before we go into more advanced development of custom tools for the Processing toolbox, and you will learn how to create your own plugins.

Getting to know the Python console

The most direct way to interact with the QGIS API is through the Python console, which can be opened by going to **Plugins** | **Python Console**. As you can see in the following screenshot the, **Python Console** is displayed within a new panel below the map:

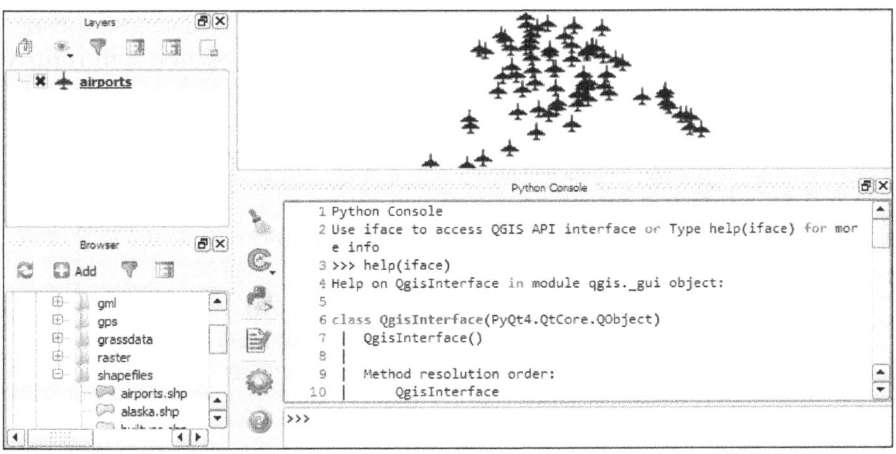

Our access point to interact with the application, project, and data is the `iface` object. To get a list of all the functions available for `iface`, type `help(iface)`. Alternatively, this information is also available online in the API documentation at `http://qgis.org/api/classQgisInterface.html`.

Loading and exploring datasets

One of the first things we want to do is to load some data. For example, to load a vector layer, we will use the `addVectorLayer()` function of `iface`:

```
v_layer = iface.addVectorLayer('C:/Users/Anita/Geodaten/qgis_sample_
data/shapefiles/airports.shp','airports','ogr')
```

When we execute this command, `airports.shp` is loaded using the `ogr` driver and added to the map under the `airports` layer name. Additionally, this function returns the created layer object. Using this layer object, which we stored in `v_layer`, we can access the vector layer functions, such as `name()`, which returns the layer name as it is displayed in the **Layers** list:

```
v_layer.name()
Output -
u'airports'
```

(The `u` in front of the `airports` layer name shows that the name is returned as a Unicode string.) Of course, the next logical step is to look at the layer's features. The number of features can be accessed using `featureCount()`:

```
v_layer.featureCount()
Output -
76L
```

This shows us that the airport layer contains 76 features. The `L` in the end shows that it's a numerical value of type `long`. In our next step, we will access these features. This is possible using the `getFeatures()` function, which will return a `QgsFeatureIterator` object. With a simple `for` loop, we can then print out `attributes()` of all the features in our layer:

```
my_features = v_layer.getFeatures()
for feature in my_features:
    print feature.attributes()
Output -
[1, u'US00157', 78.0, u'Airport/Airfield', u'PA', u'NOATAK' ...
[2, u'US00229', 264.0, u'Airport/Airfield', u'PA', u'AMBLER'...
[3, u'US00186', 585.0, u'Airport/Airfield', u'PABT', u'BETTL...
...
```

When using the preceding code snippet, it is worth noting that the Python syntax requires proper indentation. This means that, for example, the content of the `for` loop has to be indented as shown in the preceding code. If Python encounters such errors, it will raise an **IndentationError**.

You might have noticed that `attributes()` shows us the attribute values, but we don't know the field names yet. To get these names, we use:

```
for field in v_layer.dataProvider().fields():
    print field.name()
Output-
cat
NA3
ELEV
F_CODE
IKO
NAME
USE
```

Once we know the field names, we can access specific feature attributes, for example, `NAME`:

```
for feature in v_layer.getFeatures():
    print feature.attribute('NAME')
Output-
NOATAK
AMBLER
BETTLES
...
```

A quick solution to, for example, sum up the elevation values is:

```
sum([feature.attribute('ELEV') for feature in v_layer.getFeatures()])
Output-
22758.0
```

In the previous example, we took advantage of the fact that Python allows us to create a list by writing a `for` loop inside square brackets. This is called **list comprehension**, and you can read more about it at `https://docs.python.org/2/tutorial/datastructures.html#list-comprehensions`.

Loading raster data is very similar to loading vector data and is done using `addRasterLayer()`:

```
r_layer = iface.addRasterLayer('C:/Users/Anita/Geodaten/qgis_sample_
data/raster/SR_50M_alaska_nad.tif','hillshade')
r_layer.name()
Output -
u'hillshade'
```

To get the raster layer's size in pixels, we can use the `width()` and `height()` functions:

```
r_layer.width(), r_layer.height()
Output -
(1754, 1394)
```

If we want to know more about the raster values, we will use the layer's data provider object, which provides access to the raster band statistics. It's worth noting that we have to use `bandStatistics(1)` instead of `bandStatistics(0)` to access the statistics of a single-band raster, such as our `hillshade` layer, for the maximum value:

```
r_layer.dataProvider().bandStatistics(1).maximumValue
Output -
251.0
```

Other values that can be accessed like this are, for example, `minimumValue`, `range`, `stdDev`, and `sum`. For a full list, use:

```
help(r_layer.dataProvider().bandStatistics(1))
```

Styling layers

Since we now know how to load data, we can continue to style the layers. The simplest option is to load a premade style (the `.qml` file):

```
v_layer.loadNamedStyle('C:/temp/planes.qml')
```

> You can create `planes.qml` by saving the airport style we created in *Chapter 2, Viewing Spatial Data,* (just go to **Layer Properties** | **Style** | **Save Style** | **QGIS Layer Style File**), or you can use any other style you like.

Of course, we can also create a style in code. Let's have a look at a basic single-symbol renderer. We will create a simple symbol with one layer, for example, a yellow diamond:

```
from PyQt4.QtGui import QColor
```

```
symbol = QgsMarkerSymbolV2()
symbol.symbolLayer(0).setName('diamond')
symbol.symbolLayer(0).setSize(10)
symbol.symbolLayer(0).setColor(QColor('#ffff00'))
v_layer.rendererV2().setSymbol(symbol)
```

A much more advanced approach is to create a rule-based renderer. We discussed the basics of rule-based renderers in *Chapter 5, Creating Great Maps*. The following example creates two rules: one for civil-use airports and one for all the other airports. Each rule in this example has a name, a filter expression, and a symbol color. Note how the rules are appended to the renderer's root rule:

```
from PyQt4.QtGui import QColor
rules = [['Civil','USE LIKE \'%Civil%\'','green'], ['Other','USE NOT
LIKE \'%Civil%\'','red']]
symbol = QgsSymbolV2.defaultSymbol(v_layer.geometryType())
renderer = QgsRuleBasedRendererV2(symbol)
root_rule = renderer.rootRule()
for label, expression, color_name in rules:
    rule = root_rule.children()[0].clone()
    rule.setLabel(label)
    rule.setFilterExpression(expression)
    rule.symbol().setColor(QColor(color_name))
    root_rule.appendChild(rule)
root_rule.removeChildAt(0)
v_layer.setRendererV2(renderer)
```

Due to the length of this script, I recommend that you use the **Python Console** editor, which you can open by clicking on the **Show editor** button, as shown in the following screenshot:

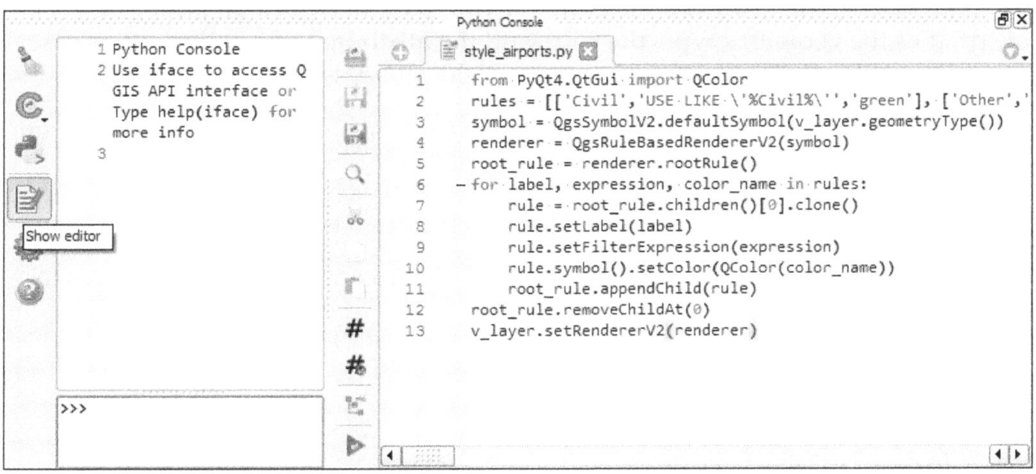

To run the script, click on the **Run script** button at the bottom of the editor toolbar.

> If you are interested in reading more about styling vector layers, I would recommend Joshua Arnott's post at `http://snorf.net/blog/2014/03/04/symbology-of-vector-layers-in-qgis-python-plugins/`.

Filtering data

To filter vector layer features programmatically, we can specify a subset string. This is the same as defining a **Feature subset** query by going to **Layer Properties** | **General**. For example, we can choose to display airports only if their name starts with `A`:

```
v_layer.setSubsetString("NAME LIKE 'A%'")
```

To remove the filter, just set an empty subset string:

```
v_layer.setSubsetString("")
```

Creating a memory layer

A great way to create a temporary vector layer is to use the so-called **memory layers**. Memory layers are a good option for temporary analysis output or visualizations. They exist within a QGIS session and are destroyed when QGIS is closed. In the following example, we will create a memory layer and add a polygon feature to it.

Basically, a memory layer is a `QgsVectorLayer` like any other layer; however, the provider (the third parameter) is not "`ogr`" like in the previous example of loading a file, but "`memory`". Instead of a file path, the first parameter is a definition string that specifies the geometry type, the CRS, and the attribute table fields (in this case, one integer field called `MYNUM` and one string field called `MYTXT`):

```
mem_layer = QgsVectorLayer("Polygon?crs=epsg:4326&field=MYNUM:integer&
field=MYTXT:string", "temp_layer", "memory")
if not mem_layer.isValid():
    raise Exception("Failed to create memory layer")
```

Once we have created the `QgsVectorLayer` object, we can start adding features to its data provider:

```
mem_layer_provider = mem_layer.dataProvider()
my_polygon = QgsFeature()
my_polygon.setGeometry(QgsGeometry.fromRect(QgsRectang
le(16,48,17,49)))
```

```
my_polygon.setAttributes([10,"hello world"])
mem_layer_provider.addFeatures([my_polygon])
QgsMapLayerRegistry.instance().addMapLayer(mem_layer)
```

Note how we first created a blank `QgsFeature` parameter to which we then added geometry and attributes using `setGeometry()` and `setAttributes()`, respectively. When we add the layer to `QgsMapLayerRegistry`, the layer is rendered on the map.

Exporting map images

The simplest option to save the current map is to use the scripting equivalent of **Project | Save as image**. This will export the current map to an image file of the same resolution as the map area in the QGIS application window:

```
iface.mapCanvas().saveAsImage('C:/temp/simple_export.png')
```

When we want to have more control over the size and resolution of the exported image, we will need a few more lines of code. The following example show how we can create our own `QgsMapRendererCustomPainterJob` object and configure it to our liking using custom `QgsMapSettings` for size (`width` and `height`), resolution (`dpi`), map `extent`, and map `layers`:

```
from PyQt4.QtGui import QImage, QPainter
from PyQt4.QtCore import QSize
# configure the output image
width = 800
height = 600
dpi = 92
img = QImage(QSize(width, height), QImage.Format_RGB32)
img.setDotsPerMeterX(dpi / 25.4 * 1000)
img.setDotsPerMeterY(dpi / 25.4 * 1000)
# get the map layers and extent
layers = [ layer.id() for layer in iface.legendInterface().layers() ]
extent = iface.mapCanvas().extent()
# configure map settings for export
mapSettings = QgsMapSettings()
mapSettings.setMapUnits(0)
mapSettings.setExtent(extent)
mapSettings.setOutputDpi(dpi)
mapSettings.setOutputSize(QSize(width, height))
mapSettings.setLayers(layers)
mapSettings.setFlags(QgsMapSettings.Antialiasing | QgsMapSettings.
UseAdvancedEffects | QgsMapSettings.ForceVectorOutput |
QgsMapSettings.DrawLabeling)
# configure and run painter
```

```
p = QPainter()
p.begin(img)
mapRenderer = QgsMapRendererCustomPainterJob(mapSettings, p)
mapRenderer.start()
mapRenderer.waitForFinished()
p.end()
# save the result
img.save("C:/temp/custom_export.png","png")
```

Creating custom geoprocessing scripts using Python

In *Chapter 4, Spatial Analysis,* we already used the existing tools in the **Processing toolbox** to analyze our data, but we are not limited to these tools. We can expand processing with our own scripts. The advantages of processing scripts over normal Python scripts, like the ones we saw in the previous section, are:

- Processing automatically generates a graphical user interface for the script to configure the script's parameters
- Processing scripts can be used in the **Graphical modeler** to create geoprocessing models

A good resource to learn how to write custom scripts for processing is to have a look at the existing scripts in the **Scripts** section in the **Processing Toolbox**. As the following screenshot shows, you can access the source code of all the existing scripts through the context menu entry **Edit script**:

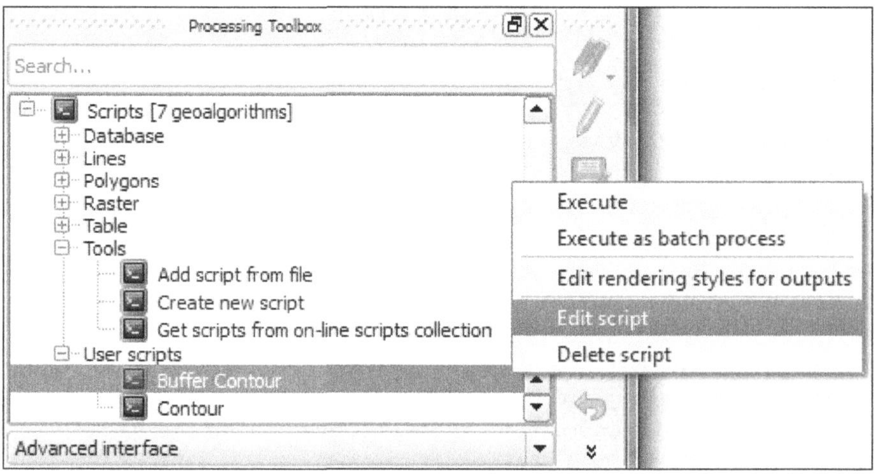

Writing our first processing script

We will create our first simple script that fetches some layer information. To get started, double-click on the **Create new script** entry by navigating to **Scripts** | **Tools**. This will open an empty editor dialog. The following screenshot shows the editor with a short script that prints the input layer's name to the **Python Console**:

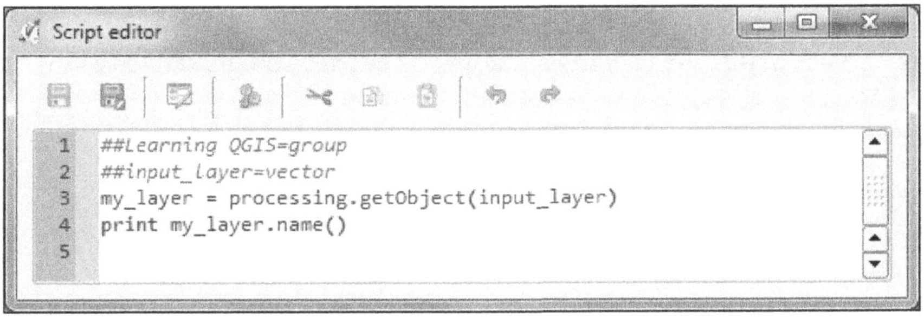

The first line defines that our script will be put into the Learning QGIS group of scripts, as shown in the following screenshot. The double hashes, `##`, are the Processing syntax. They indicate that the line contains Processing-specific information rather than Python code. The script name is created from the filename you chose when saving the script. For this example, I saved the script as `my_first_script.py`. The second line defines the script input, in this case, a vector layer. In the following line, we use Processing's `getObject()` function to get access to the input layer object, and finally, the layer name is printed to the **Python Console**. You can either run the script directly from within the editor by clicking on the **Run algorithm** button or by double-clicking on the entry in the **Processing Toolbox**:

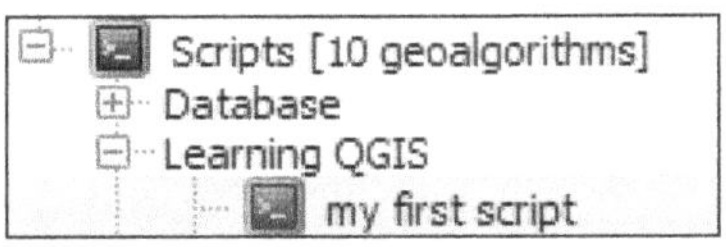

Writing a script with vector layer output

Of course, in most cases, we don't want to just output something in the **Python Console**. That is why the following example shows how to create a vector layer. More specifically, the script creates square polygons around input points. The numeric `size` input parameter controls the size of the squares in the `output vector` layer. The default size that will be displayed in the automatically generated dialog is setto `1000000`:

```
##Learning QGIS=group
##input_layer=vector
```

```
##size=number 1000000
##squares=output vector
from qgis.core import *
from processing.core.VectorWriter import VectorWriter
# get the input layer and its fields
my_layer = processing.getObject(input_layer)
fields = my_layer.dataProvider().fields()
# create the output vector writer with the same fields
writer = VectorWriter(squares, None, fields, QGis.WKBPolygon, my_
layer.crs())
# create output features
feat = QgsFeature()
for input_feature in my_layer.getFeatures():
  # copy attributes from the input point feature
  attributes = input_feature.attributes()
  feat.setAttributes(attributes)
  # create square polygons
  point = input_feature.geometry().asPoint()
  xmin = point.x() - size/2
  ymin = point.y() - size/2
  square = QgsRectangle(xmin,ymin,xmin+size,ymin+size)
  feat.setGeometry(QgsGeometry.fromRect(square))
  writer.addFeature(feat)
del writer
```

In this script, we used `VectorWriter` to write the output vector layer. The parameters used to create `VectorWriter` are `fileName`, `encoding`, `fields`, `geometryType`, and `crs`. The available geometry types are `QGis.WKBPoint`, `QGis.WKBLineString`, `QGis.WKBPolygon`,`QGis.WKBMultiPoint`, and `QGis.WKBMultiLineString`, and `QGis.WKBMultiPolygon`. You can also get this list of geometry types by typing `VectorWriter.TYPE_MAP` in the **Python Console**.

Note how we used the fields of the input layer (`my_layer.dataProvider().fields()`) input to create the `VectorWriter`. This ensures that the output layer has the same fields (attribute table columns) as the input layer. Similarly, for each feature in the input layer, we copied its attribute values (`input_feature.attributes()`) to the corresponding output feature.

After running the script, the resulting layer will be loaded into QGIS and listed using the output parameter name; in this case, the layer is called `squares`. The following screenshot shows the automatically generated input dialog as well as the output of the script when applied to the airports from our sample dataset:

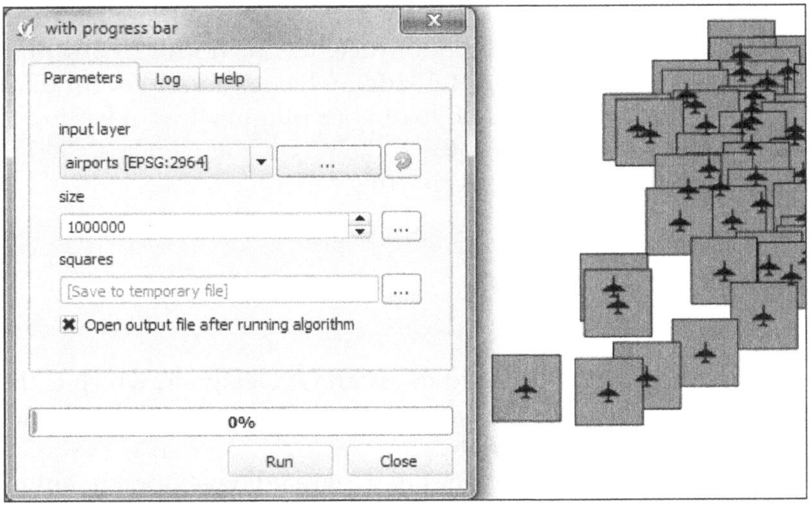

Visualizing the script progress

Especially when executing complex scripts that take a while to finish, it is a good practice to display the progress of the script execution in a progress bar. To add a progress bar to the previous script, we can add the following lines of code before and inside the `for` loop, which loops through the input features:

```
i = 0
n = my_layer.featureCount()
for input_feature in my_layer.getFeatures():
    progress.setPercentage(int(100*i/n))
    i+=1
```

Note that we initialized the counter `i` before the loop and increased it inside the loop after updating the progress bar using `progress.setPercentage()`.

Developing your first plugin

When you want to implement interactive tools or very specific graphical user interfaces, it is time to look into plugin development. In the previous exercises, we already introduced the QGIS Python API. Therefore, we can now focus on the necessary steps to get your first QGIS plugin started. A great thing about creating plugins for QGIS is that there is a plugin for this! It's called **Plugin Builder**. And while you are at it, also install **Plugin Reloader**, which is a very useful plugin for developers because it lets you quickly reload your plugin without having to restart QGIS every time you make changes to the code. When you have installed both plugins, your **Plugins** toolbar will look like this:

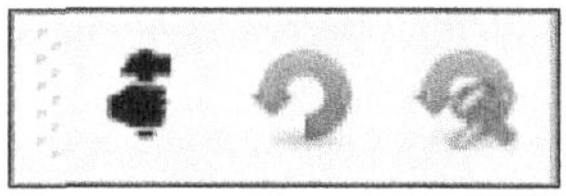

Before we can get started, you also need to install **Qt Designer**, which is the application we will use to design the user interface. If you are using Windows, I suggest that you install **WinPython** (`http://winpython.sourceforge.net/`), which provides Qt Designer and **Spyder** (an integrated development environment for Python). On Ubuntu, you can install Qt Designer using `sudo apt-get install qt4-designer`. On Mac, you can get the **Qt Creator** installer, which includes Qt Designer, from `http://qt-project.org/downloads`.

Creating the plugin template with Plugin Builder

Plugin Builder will create all the files we need for our plugin. Just start **Plugin Builder** and input the class name (one word in CamelCase, that is, each word starts with an uppercase letter with no spaces between the words) as well as **Plugin name**, a short **Description**, and **Module name** (the Python module name for the plugin). Also fill in the **Text for the menu item** field. When you hover your mouse over the input fields in the **QGIS Plugin Builder** dialog box, it displays help information, as shown in the following screenshot:

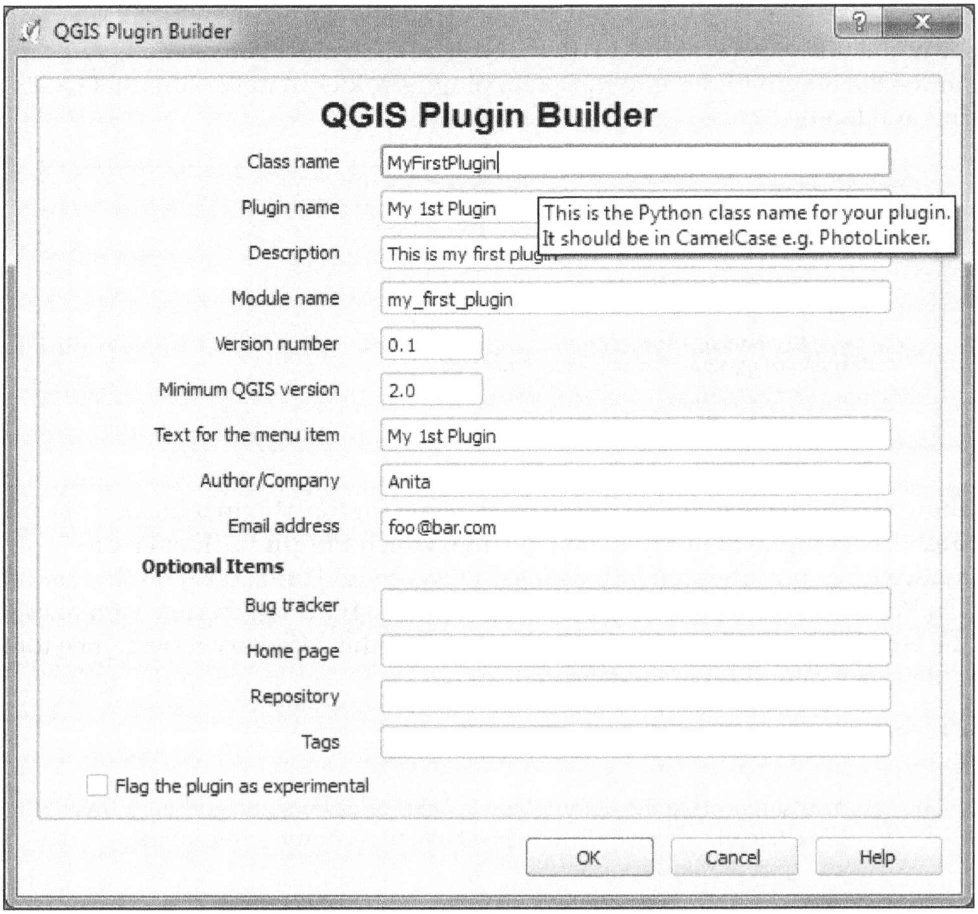

Since we are only planning to create the first plugin for learning purposes, we can skip the **Optional Items** section at the bottom of the dialog. If you later create a plugin that you might want to share with other users on the QGIS plugin repository, you should also fill in these items to provide future users of your plugin with details regarding where to find information about the plugin or where to report issues.

Once you click on **OK**, you're asked to select a folder to store the plugin. You can save it directly to the QGIS plugin folder `~\.qgis2\python\plugins` QGIS plugin folder on Windows or `~/.qgis2/python/plugins` on Linux and Mac. When you have selected the plugin folder, it displays a confirmation **Plugin Builder Results** dialog, which confirms the location of your plugin folder as well as the location of your QGIS plugin folder.

As mentioned earlier, I saved the plugin directly to the QGIS plugin folder, as you can see in the following screenshot. If you saved it in a different location, you can now move the plugin folder into the QGIS plugins folder to make sure that QGIS can find and load it.

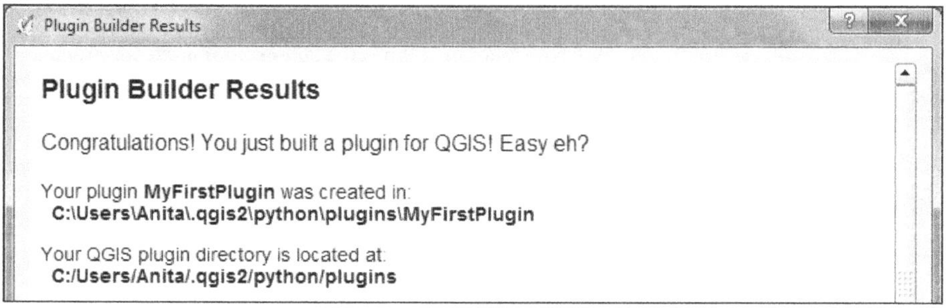

One thing we still have to do is to prepare the icon for the plugin toolbar. This requires us to compile the `resources.qrc` file, which **Plugin Builder** created automatically, to turn the icon into usable Python code. This is done on the command line. On Windows, I suggest that you use the **OSGeo4W Shell**, because it makes sure that the environment variables are set in a way that the necessary tools can be found. Navigate to the plugin folder and run:

```
pyrcc4 -o resources_rc.py resources.qrc
```

> You can replace the default icon (`icon.png`) image to add your own plugin icon. Afterwards, you just have to recompile `resources_rc.qrc`, as shown earlier.

Restart QGIS and you should now see your plugin listed in the Plugin Manager, as shown here:

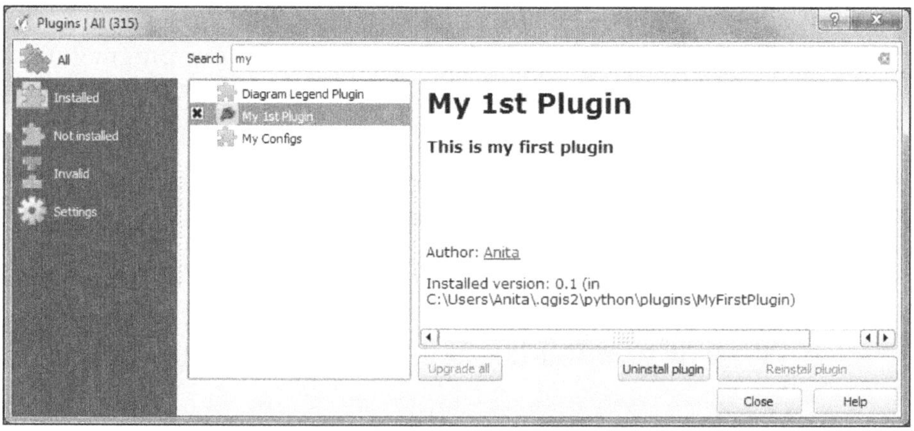

Activate your plugin in the **Plugin** manager and you should see it listed in the **Plugins** menu. When you start your plugin, it will display a blank dialog that is just waiting for you to customize it.

Customizing the plugin GUI

To customize the blank default plugin dialog, we will now use Qt Designer. You find the dialog file in the plugin folder; in my case, it is called `my_first_plugin_dialog_base.ui` (derived from the module name I specified in **Plugin Builder**). When you open your plugin `.ui` file in Qt Designer, you will see a blank dialog. Now you can start adding widgets by dragging-and-dropping them from the **Widget Box** on the left-hand side of the Qt Designer window. In the following screenshot, you can see that I added a **Label** and a drop-down list widget (listed as **Combo Box** in **Widget Box**). You can change the label text to `Layer` by double-clicking on the default label text. Additionally, it is a good practice to assign descriptive names to the widget objects, for example, I renamed the combo box to `layerCombo`, as you can see in the following screenshot:

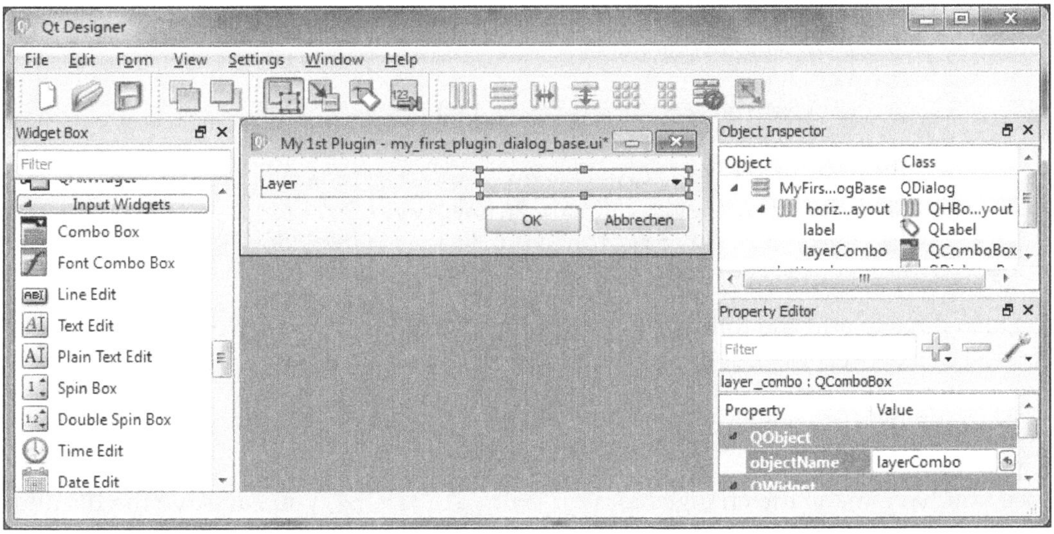

Once you have made the changes to the plugin dialog, you can save them. Then, you can go back to QGIS. In QGIS, you can then configure the plugin reloader by clicking on the **Choose a plugin to be reloaded** button in the **Plugins** toolbar and selecting your plugin. If you now click on the **Reload Plugin** button and then start your plugin, your new plugin dialog will be displayed.

Implementing the plugin functionality

As you have certainly noticed, the combobox layer is still empty. To populate the combobox with a list of the loaded layers, we need to add a few lines of code in `my_first_plugin.py` (located in the plugin folder). More specifically, we will expand the `run()` method:

```
def run(self):
    """Run method that performs all the real work"""
    # show the dialog
    self.dlg.show()
    # clear the combo box to list only current layers
    self.dlg.layerCombo.clear()
    # get the layers and add them to the combo box
    layers = QgsMapLayerRegistry.instance().mapLayers().values()
    for layer in layers:
        if layer.type() == QgsMapLayer.VectorLayer:
            self.dlg.layerCombo.addItem( layer.name(), layer )
    # Run the dialog event loop
    result = self.dlg.exec_()
    # See if OK was pressed
    if result:
        # Check which layer was selected
        index = self.dlg.layerCombo.currentIndex()
        layer = self.dlg.layerCombo.itemData(index)
        # Display information about the layer
        QMessageBox.information(self.iface.mainWindow(),"Learning
QGIS","%s has %d features." %(layer.name(),layer.featureCount()))
```

You also have to add the following import line at the top of the script to avoid `NameErrors` concerning `QgsMapLayerRegistry` and `QMessageBox`:

```
from qgis.core import *
from PyQt4.QtGui import QMessageBox
```

Once you have made the changes to `my_first_plugin.py`, you can save the file and use the **Reload Plugin** button in QGIS to reload your plugin. If you start your plugin now, the combobox will be populated with a list of all the layers in the current QGIS project, and when you click on **OK**, you will see a message box that displays the number of features in the selected layer.

Creating a custom map tool

While the previous exercise showed how to create a custom GUI that enables the user to interact with QGIS, in this exercise, we will go one step further and implement our own custom **map tool** similar to the default **Identify** tool. This means that the user can click on the map and the tool reports which feature on the map was clicked.

To this end, we will create another default plugin template called `MyFirstMapTool`. For this tool, we do not need to create a dialog. Instead, we have to write a bit more code than we did in the previous example. First, we create our custom map tool class, which we call `IdentifyFeatureTool`. Besides the `__init__()` constructor, this tool has one function called `canvasReleaseEvent()`, which defines the actions of the tool when the mouse button is released (that is, when you let go of the mouse button after pressing it down):

```
class IdentifyFeatureTool(QgsMapToolIdentify):
    def __init__(self, canvas):
        QgsMapToolIdentify.__init__(self, canvas)
    def canvasReleaseEvent(self, mouseEvent):
        print "canvasReleaseEvent"
        # get features at the current mouse position
        results = self.identify(mouseEvent.x(),mouseEvent.y(),
                        self.TopDownStopAtFirst, self.VectorLayer)
        if len(results) > 0:
            # signal that a feature was identified
            self.emit( SIGNAL( "geomIdentified" ),
                       results[0].mLayer, results[0].mFeature)
```

You can paste the preceding code at the end of the `my_first_map_tool.py` file. Of course, we now have to put our new map tool to good use. In the `initGui()` function, we replace the `run()` method with a new `map_tool_init()` function. Additionally, we define that our map tool is checkable; this means that the user can click on the tool icon to activate it and click on it again to deactivate it:

```
def initGui(self):
    # create the toolbar icon and menu entry
    icon_path = ':/plugins/MyFirstMapTool/icon.png'
    self.map_tool_action=self.add_action(
        icon_path,
        text=self.tr(u'My 1st Map Tool'),
        callback=self.map_tool_init,
        parent=self.iface.mainWindow())
    self.map_tool_action.setCheckable(True)
```

The new `map_tool_init()` function takes care of activating or deactivating our map tool when the button is clicked. During activation, it creates an instance of our custom `IdentifyFeatureTool` and the following line connects the map tool's `geomIdentified` signal to the `do_something()` function, which we will discuss in a moment. Similarly, when the map tool is deactivated, we disconnect the signal and restore the previous map tool:

```
def map_tool_init(self):
    # this function is called when the map tool icon is clicked
    print "maptoolinit"
    canvas = self.iface.mapCanvas()
    if self.map_tool_action.isChecked():
        # when the user activates the tool
        self.prev_tool = canvas.mapTool()
        self.map_tool_action.setChecked( True )
        self.map_tool = IdentifyFeatureTool(canvas)
        QObject.connect(self.map_tool, SIGNAL("geomIdentified"),
                        self.do_something )
        canvas.setMapTool(self.map_tool)
        QObject.connect(canvas,SIGNAL("mapToolSet(QgsMapTool *)"),
                        self.map_tool_changed)
    else:
        # when the user deactivates the tool
        QObject.disconnect( canvas, SIGNAL( "mapToolSet(QgsMapTool *)"
                            ),self.map_tool_changed)
        canvas.unsetMapTool(self.map_tool)
        print "restore prev tool %s" %(self.prev_tool)
        canvas.setMapTool(self.prev_tool)
```

Our new custom `do_something()` function is called when our map tool was used to successfully identify a feature. For this example, we simply print the feature's attributes to the **Python Console**. Of course, you can get creative here and add your desired custom functionality:

```
def do_something(self, layer, feature):
    print feature.attributes()
```

Finally, we also have to handle the case when the user switches to a different map tool. This is similar to the case of the user deactivating our tool in the `map_tool_init()` function:

```
def map_tool_changed(self):
    print "maptoolchanged"
    canvas = self.iface.mapCanvas()
    QObject.disconnect(canvas, SIGNAL("mapToolSet(QgsMapTool *)"),
                       self.map_tool_changed)
```

```
        canvas.unsetMapTool(self.map_tool)
        self.map_tool_action.setChecked(False)
```

You also have to add the following import line at the top of the script to avoid errors concerning `QObject`, `QgsMapTool`, and others:

```
from qgis.core import *
from qgis.gui import *
from PyQt4.QtCore import *
```

When you are ready, you can reload the plugin and try it. You should have the **Python Console** open to be able to follow the plugin's outputs. The first thing you will see when you activate the plugin in the toolbar is that it prints `maptoolinit` to the console. Then, if you click inside the map, it will print `canvasReleaseEvent`, and if you click on a feature, it will also display the feature's attributes. Finally, if you change to another map tool (for example, to the **Pan Map** tool), it will print `maptoolchanged` to the console and the icon in the plugin toolbar will be unchecked.

Summary

In this chapter, we covered different ways to extend QGIS using Python scripting. We started with the **Python Console**, which offers a direct interactive way to interact with the QGIS Python API. We also used the editor that is part of the **Python Console** panel and provides a better way to work on longer scripts that contain loops or even multiple class and function definitions. Next, we applied our knowledge of PyQGIS to develop custom tools for the **Processing Toolbox**. These tools profit from Processing's automatic GUI-generation capabilities, and they can be used in the **Graphical** modeler to create geopreocessing models. Last but not least, we developed a basic plugin based on a **Plugin Builder** template.

With this information, you can now start your own PyQGIS experiments. There are multiple web and print resources that you can use to learn more about QGIS Python scripting. For the updated QGIS API documentation, check out `http://qgis.org/api/`. If you are interested in more PyQGIS recipes, have a look at the *PyQGIS Developer Cookbook* at `http://docs.qgis.org/testing/en/docs/pyqgis_developer_cookbook` and *QGIS Cookbook, Packt Publishing*, which will be out soon. For a more in-depth look into PyQGIS, with further examples, tips, and an introduction to writing stand-alone applications using PyQGIS, I recommend Gary Sherman's book, *The PyQGIS Programmer's Guide, Locate Press*.

Index

A

B

C

M

N

O

P

Q

R

S

T

[PACKT] open source
community experience distilled
PUBLISHING

Thank you for buying

Learning QGIS
Second Edition

About Packt Publishing

Packt, pronounced 'packed', published its first book, *Mastering phpMyAdmin for Effective MySQL Management*, in April 2004, and subsequently continued to specialize in publishing highly focused books on specific technologies and solutions.

Our books and publications share the experiences of your fellow IT professionals in adapting and customizing today's systems, applications, and frameworks. Our solution-based books give you the knowledge and power to customize the software and technologies you're using to get the job done. Packt books are more specific and less general than the IT books you have seen in the past. Our unique business model allows us to bring you more focused information, giving you more of what you need to know, and less of what you don't.

Packt is a modern yet unique publishing company that focuses on producing quality, cutting-edge books for communities of developers, administrators, and newbies alike. For more information, please visit our website at `www.packtpub.com`.

About Packt Open Source

In 2010, Packt launched two new brands, Packt Open Source and Packt Enterprise, in order to continue its focus on specialization. This book is part of the Packt Open Source brand, home to books published on software built around open source licenses, and offering information to anybody from advanced developers to budding web designers. The Open Source brand also runs Packt's Open Source Royalty Scheme, by which Packt gives a royalty to each open source project about whose software a book is sold.

Writing for Packt

We welcome all inquiries from people who are interested in authoring. Book proposals should be sent to `author@packtpub.com`. If your book idea is still at an early stage and you would like to discuss it first before writing a formal book proposal, then please contact us; one of our commissioning editors will get in touch with you.

We're not just looking for published authors; if you have strong technical skills but no writing experience, our experienced editors can help you develop a writing career, or simply get some additional reward for your expertise.

[PACKT] open source
community experience distilled
PUBLISHING

PostGIS Cookbook

ISBN: 978-1-84951-866-6 Paperback: 484 pages

Over 80 task-based recipes to store, organize, manipulate, and analyze spatial data in a PostGIS database

1. Integrate PostGIS with web frameworks and implement OGC standards such as WMS and WFS using MapServer and GeoServer.
2. Convert 2D and 3D vector data, raster data, and routing data into usable forms.
3. Visualize data from the PostGIS database using a desktop GIS program such as QGIS and OpenJUMP.

Programming ArcGIS 10.1 with Python Cookbook

ISBN: 978-1-84969-444-5 Paperback: 304 pages

Over 75 recipes to help you automate geoprocessing tasks, create solutions, and solve problems for ArcGIS with Python

1. Learn how to create geoprocessing scripts with ArcPy.
2. Customize and modify ArcGIS with Python.
3. Create time-saving tools and scripts for ArcGIS.

Please check **www.PacktPub.com** for information on our titles

Lightning Source UK Ltd.
Milton Keynes UK
UKOW07f1015120515

251326UK00007B/133/P

9 781784 392031